BRIEF INTERVENTION
FOR SCHOOL PROBLEMS

The Guilford School Practitioner Series

EDITORS

STEPHEN N. ELLIOTT, Ph.D.
University of Wisconsin–Madison

JOSEPH C. WITT, Ph.D.
Louisiana State University, Baton Rouge

Recent Volumes

Individual and Group Counseling in Schools
STEWART EHLY and RICHARD DUSTIN

School–Home Notes: Promoting Children's Classroom Success
MARY LOU KELLEY

Childhood Depression: School-Based Intervention
KEVIN D. STARK

Assessment for Early Intervention: Best Practices for Professionals
STEPHEN J. BAGNATO and JOHN T. NEISWORTH

The Clinical Child Interview
JAN N. HUGHES and DAVID B. BAKER

Working with Families in Crisis: School-Based Intervention
WILLIAM STEELE and MELVYN RAIDER

Practitioner's Guide to Dynamic Assessment
CAROL S. LIDZ

Reading Problems: Consultation and Remediation
P. G. AARON and R. MALATESHA JOSHI

Crisis Intervention in the Schools
GAYLE D. PITCHER and SCOTT POLAND

Behavior Change in the Classroom: Self-Management Interventions
EDWARD S. SHAPIRO and CHRISTINE L. COLE

ADHD in the Schools: Assessment and Intervention Strategies
GEORGE J. DuPAUL and GARY STONER

School Interventions for Children of Alcoholics
BONNIE K. NASTASI and DENISE M. DeZOLT

Entry Strategies for School Consultation
EDWARD S. MARKS

Instructional Consultation Teams: Collaborating for Change
SYLVIA A. ROSENFIELD and TODD A. GRAVOIS

Social Problem Solving: Interventions in the Schools
MAURICE J. ELIAS and STEVEN E. TOBIAS

Academic Skills Problems: Direct Assessment
and Intervention, Second Edition
EDWARD S. SHAPIRO

Brief Intervention for School Problems:
Collaborating for Practical Solutions
JOHN J. MURPHY and BARRY L. DUNCAN

Brief Intervention
for School Problems

COLLABORATING FOR PRACTICAL SOLUTIONS

♦♦♦

John J. Murphy
Barry L. Duncan

♦

THE GUILFORD PRESS
New York   London

© 1997 The Guilford Press
A Division of Guilford Publications, Inc.
72 Spring Street, New York, NY 10012

Printed in the United States of America

This book is printed on acid-free paper.

Last digit is print number: 9 8 7 6 5 4

Library of Congress Cataloging-in-Publication Data

Murphy, John J. (John Joseph), 1955–
    Brief intervention for school problems : collaborating for
practical solutions / John J. Murphy, Barry L. Duncan.
        p.   cm. — (The Guilford school practitioner series)
    Includes bibliographical references and index.
    ISBN 1-57230-174-0
    1. Problem children—Education—United States—Case studies.
2. Educational counseling—United States—Case studies.   3. Student
assistance programs—United States—Case studies.   4. Problem
children—Services for—United States—Case studies.   I. Duncan,
Barry L.   II. Title.   II. Series.
LC4802.M87   1997
371.93—DC21   96-45265
                                                        CIP

*In memory of John Murphy's father, Bob Murphy,
and Barry Duncan's father-in-law, Alf Adler*

Preface

♦

Every journey begins with a single step. Our first step toward this book occurred in 1989. John was a school psychologist in Covington (KY) Independent Public Schools, an urban district serving many at-risk students. Barry was a therapist and Director of the Dayton (OH) Institute for Family Therapy, a treatment and training facility known for accepting difficult cases.

From the time we met to arrange a postdoctoral externship for John at the Institute, it was apparent that we had much in common. First, we shared a passion for discovering what works in helping people change. Second, we worked with many students viewed as hopeless by schools, other practitioners, and themselves, *and* enjoyed it. We found "difficult" clients to be the best teachers of intervention, and learned invaluable lessons about what works and does not work in changing school problems. Third, we were full-time practitioners with a firsthand appreciation of the many constraints and challenges of working with students, parents, and teachers to resolve school problems. Neither of us had much tolerance for approaches that sounded good in theory or on paper, yet were ineffective in the real world. We were convinced that it was possible to be scientist/practitioners and to utilize empirical research findings in the daily trenches of our work lives.

Several discussions and five years later, we decided to write this book. Both of us have changed jobs and states since then. However, we have continued our journey to discover and apply what works in changing school problems. We are delighted with the opportunity to share what we have learned on the road to *Brief Intervention for School*

Problems. We have had hundreds of eye-opening experiences along the way, many of which are reported in this book. Our guiding question has been a simple, pragmatic one: "What works?" This book is our response.

The book addresses the most common type of referral for school-related counseling, consultation, or intervention—a parent or teacher expresses a concern or complaint about a student, and an accompanying desire for rapid change. Research on factors that contribute to successful intervention has been around for decades. However, the interpretation of empirical findings into user-friendly strategies for school practitioners has been sadly lacking. This book translates research on what works into a practical approach to school problems.

In conducting workshops throughout the country, we have been encouraged by numerous school practitioners to write this book. Many have expressed appreciation for the approach's practical, straightforward pursuit of change. In keeping with the pragmatic nature of brief intervention, our most important measure of the book's success will be the extent to which school practitioners apply it on the job.

Every major concept and strategy presented in this book can be applied by real practitioners to real problems of real people in the real world. Case examples are provided to bring the material to life and increase its relevance to school practitioners. Our work as full-time practitioners has made us all too aware of the demands and challenges of school-based intervention, such as time constraints, heavy caseloads, and limited availability of parents and school staff for meetings. For this reason, we adopted the following guideline in choosing what to include (and not include) in the book: *If we have not actually done it ourselves, it is not in the book.*

Brief Intervention for School Problems is intended primarily for school psychologists, counselors, therapists, social workers, students in training, and others who regularly work with school problems. The scientist/practitioner orientation of the book enhances its usefulness as a text in graduate courses on school-based intervention, counseling, and consultation. Although the book is written from a school practitioner's perspective, the ideas and strategies of brief intervention also have been well received by school administrators, teachers, and parents.

We want to clarify some terminology at the outset. The word

"client" is used in this book to refer to any person with whom the practitioner works to change a school problem, such as a student, teacher, or parent. The term "school practitioner" encompasses a wide range of professionals including school psychologists, counselors, social workers, therapists, and other practitioners involved in resolving school problems. We do not make distinctions in this book between "counseling," "consultation," and "intervention," because the common element of each of these is a request for change. "Intervention" is used throughout the book to include counseling, consultation, and any other activities involved in changing school problems.

Part 1 presents the foundations of "what works." Chapter 1 introduces the brief intervention approach through a case illustration involving a student experiencing multiple school and home problems. Chapter 2 presents the empirical foundations of effective intervention, along with case examples designed to connect research findings to specific applications for school practitioners. The chapter concludes with two major intervention guidelines derived from research on "what works" in resolving problems.

Part 2 illustrates the process of brief intervention from assessment (Chapter 3) to intervention (Chapters 4 and 5) to evaluation and maintenance (Chapter 6). Numerous excerpts from meetings with students, parents, and teachers are included in each chapter to illustrate specific ideas and methods.

In Part 3, two full-length case studies are provided to "put it all together" and demonstrate how the principles and practices of assessment, intervention, evaluation, and maintenance are integrated into a coherent, problem solving approach. Chapter 7 involves a high school special education student referred for disruptive behavior, and Chapter 8 presents a case involving a 10-year-old student referred for "school anxiety." Special challenges associated with brief intervention for school problems are discussed in Chapter 9, along with some suggestions for addressing them.

Applying the principles and practices described in this book has increased the effectiveness and enjoyment of our work. Brief intervention is not a panacea for every school problem, and we do not propose to have all the answers. However, we do provide some answers and clear guidelines for helping students, teachers, and parents resolve school problems.

Brief Intervention for School Problems integrates the most powerful factors of change into a pragmatic intervention approach. Our greatest hope is that you and your clients benefit from this approach—indeed, in our minds, the extent to which you do determines the success of the book. We also hope that as you read it you become impressed, as we continue to be, by the amazing resourcefulness of students, parents, and teachers in resolving school problems.

We are grateful to the following people for their encouragement and collaboration on other projects: Scott Miller, Mark Hubble, Cookie Cahill-Flower, Bruce Wess, Michael Walters, Pamela Dickey, Ron Bramlett, Mike Curtis, Dave Barnett, Joe Zins, and Janet Graden. We would also like to thank our colleagues from the Covington Independent Public Schools (Marilyn Hagenseker, Allen Bernard, Mary Ann Babbs, Nancy Hampel, Sawyer Hunley, and Beth Siler) and the Dayton Institute for Family Therapy (Greg Rusk, Andy Solovey, and Paul Bruening) for their influence on our ideas, as well as many good times. A debt of gratitude is owed to Victoria Lichtman for her transcription work, and to John Clemmons, Patricia Burris, and Lory Greer for their proofreading assistance. We are grateful to the University of Central Arkansas for grant funding, and to David Skotko, Chair of the Psychology and Counseling Department, and to Jim Bowman, Dean of the College of Education, for their encouragement and support of this book. We also appreciate the direction and support of Sharon Panulla, senior editor at The Guilford Press. Most of all, we thank our wives, Debbie and Karen, and our children, Tom, Erin, Maura, Jesse, and Matthew, for their inspiration, kindness, and stellar patience.

Contents

♦

PART 1   FOUNDATIONS

CHAPTER 1 *Kenny: An Introduction to What Works*   3

CHAPTER 2 *Empirical Foundations of Effective Intervention*   6
The Intervention Pie   7
A Commonsense Recipe for Effective Intervention   14
Conclusions   24

PART 2   THE BRIEF INTERVENTION APPROACH

CHAPTER 3 *Assessment: The First Interview*   27
Exploring the Client's World: Accommodating the Client's
    Frame of Reference   27
Discovering Possibilities   36
Validating the Client   38
Interviewing Families   40
Summary   42

CHAPTER 4 *Intervention I: The Client Knows Best*   44
Recognizing Client Factors   45
The Five-E Method of Exploring for, Discovering, and
    Validating Exceptions   50
Summary and Implications   60

CHAPTER 5 *Intervention II: If at First You Don't Succeed, Try*   62
Something Different
Doing More of the Same   62
Do Something Different   63
View Something Different   79
Summary and Conclusions   85

CHAPTER 6 *Evaluating and Maintaining Progress*   87
           Evaluating Progress   88
           Maintaining Progress   93
           Summary   106

PART 3   CASES AND CONCLUSIONS

CHAPTER 7 *The Case of Larry: Working with What Works*   109
           Referral and Background   109
           Assessment   110
           Intervention   121
           Evaluation of Progress   123
           Maintenance of Progress   123
           Conclusion and Discussion   128

CHAPTER 8 *The Case of Maria: When Rationality Doesn't*   130
           Make Sense
           Referral and Background   130
           Assessment   131
           Intervention   141
           Evaluation of Progress   146
           Maintenance of Progress   147
           Conclusion and Discussion   151

CHAPTER 9 *Special Challenges and Final Thoughts*   153
           Special Challenges   153
           Brief Intervention in a Nutshell: The 3 C's
              and 3 A's   156
           Last Call for the Client   156

APPENDIX   *Useful Interventions*   157

REFERENCES   163

INDEX   169

BRIEF INTERVENTION
FOR SCHOOL PROBLEMS

PART 1

◆◆◆

FOUNDATIONS

◆

CHAPTER 1

♦♦♦

Kenny: An Introduction to What Works

♦

Several years ago, a third-grade student named Kenny was referred to the school practitioner by his teacher for an evaluation. When asked about his family during a routine initial interview, he reported that his father had been murdered when Kenny was 5 years old. He had been removed from his mother's custody when he was 6 and placed with his aunt. An older brother was in jail for burglary. It was Kenny's third school in as many years, and his aunt was preparing to move again. The practitioner had heard similar stories from other students, but his reaction to this one was different.

Amid the usual reactions of sadness and hopelessness in response to such information, the practitioner was struck by the courage and stamina of this youngster. After a long silence following Kenny's narrative about his family, the practitioner wondered aloud how someone so young had withstood such adversity and asked, "With all the stuff that's happened in your life, how do you manage to keep hanging in there, coming to school and trying to do the schoolwork?" Kenny replied, "My aunt always tells me to never give up because quitters don't make it."

When asked about other things that helped him in school, he said that one of his older brothers occasionally assisted him with homework. Kenny added that it took him longer than other students to do math work, and that it helped when his teacher gave him extra time. After a few minutes, the situation did not seem nearly as hopeless to either of them. One small question shifted the conversation from "admiring the problem" to exploring solutions.

Following Kenny's lead, the practitioner worked to develop interventions aimed at doing "more of" what already worked to improve his school performance. His teacher agreed to provide additional opportunities for extra time in math. His brother increased from monthly to weekly visits to help him with homework. A peer-tutoring arrangement was established with an older student at school. Kenny's teacher began offering words of encouragement like those of his aunt. He was encouraged to apply similar self-affirmations in difficult situations at school. Although he struggled academically, his grades and behavior improved and he passed to the next grade.

Kenny provided all the necessary material for intervention. The school improvement strategies reflected *his* ideas and judgments, not the practitioner's. He proved a most able "consultant" when given the opportunity to explore and discover his resources. Because the school practitioner did not have any better ideas at the time, it was easy to stay out of Kenny's way as he described things that improved school performance. The practitioner's dumbfounded silence provided the opportunity for a new conversational path— a path of hope and solution. Kenny led the way by supplying the ideas. The practitioner followed by connecting these ideas to school and home intervention strategies. In short, Kenny successfully directed the change process.

The practitioner was intrigued by how change occurred in this case. Usually, he racked his brain to design and sell *his* interventions. This time, the student designed his own strategies in response to variations of the question "What do *you* think would help you in school?" The practitioner had accidentally stumbled upon a unique and powerful approach to problem solving in schools. His initial lack of intervention ideas provided the opportunity for Kenny to discover his own resources for improving school performance. As a result, the interventions were Kenny's own and required no sales job. No wonder they worked.

The case of Kenny illustrates some valuable lessons:

1. *Students are valuable intervention consultants.* As the "targets" of most school-based interventions, students are in an optimal position

to educate us on what will (and will not) work with them . . . *if we would only ask.* The same is true of parents and teachers. This book describes several ways of asking for and cooperating with the opinions and "theories" of students, parents, and teachers throughout the intervention process.

2. *Students, parents, and teachers often have the ideas, competencies, and resources required to resolve their school problems.* Kenny had already discovered "what worked" in improving school performance. However, it is doubtful that those ideas and resources would have found their way into school interventions had the practitioner not asked Kenny about them. This book provides a strong empirical rationale, along with various strategies, for assessing and utilizing client competencies and resources.

3. *Big problems do not always require big solutions.* A small change in the perception or performance of a school problem ripples into larger changes. The significant overall improvement in Kenny's school performance resulted from a combination of smaller changes. This book illustrates strategies for expanding small changes into larger ones.

4. *Important and lasting changes in school problems can occur quickly.* This is a source of great encouragement for school practitioners, who may have only one or two opportunities to meet on a school problem. Effective interventions were developed during about 30 minutes of conversation with Kenny. This book demonstrates that every contact with students, teachers, and parents is an opportunity for change.

In the next chapter, we examine the foundations of intervention with a practical emphasis on "what works" in changing school problems.

CHAPTER 2

◆◆◆

Empirical Foundations of Effective Intervention

◆

The foolish reject what they see, not
what they think; the wise reject what
they think, not what they see.
                    —HUANG PO

Research on intervention effectiveness has either bored or intimidated generations of practitioners. Besides being almost unreadable, there is little to engage the day-to-day interest of school practitioners. All that is beginning to change. We now know that the secret of Kenny's success has been identified, quantified, and described. This chapter presents the research regarding change and demonstrates its relevance to school-based practice.

Figure 2.1 is an illustration of what research suggests about the factors leading to change, that is, what works (adapted from Lambert, 1992). The research depicted in Figure 2.1 is extensive, decades old, and deals with a broad range of human problems across a variety of settings. It represents thousands of clients and hundreds of practitioners. An inspection of Figure 2.1 reveals the percentage contribution to change of four factors: (1) client factors (40%), (2) relationship factors (30%), (3) placebo factors (15%), and (4) model factors (15%).

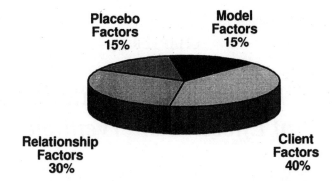

Placebo Factors 15%   **Model Factors 15%**

Relationship Factors 30%   **Client Factors 40%**

FIGURE 2.1. The intervention pie: Factors contributing to successful outcome (data from Lambert, 1992).

THE INTERVENTION PIE

Think of effective intervention as your favorite pie. Corresponding to the four factors listed above, your pie has four essential ingredients.

The Filling: Client Factors

The main ingredient to any pie is the filling, whether it is chocolate, lemon, custard, or rhubarb. The filling in this pie represents change that can be attributed to *client factors* because, at 40%, client factors represent the largest contribution to the change process. Intervening without a dependence on the client's resources is like eating a pie without filling. Researchers define client factors as those factors that are a part of the client and his or her environment (Lambert, 1992). These factors include the client's strengths, resources, innate capacities for growth, and abilities to enlist support and help from others. Kenny is a prime example of client factors at work.

Consider Molly, a delightful and precocious 10-year-old who sought help because of nightmares and an inability to sleep in her room. The problem persisted for 1 year despite two separate intervention attempts. The third practitioner asked Molly what she thought would be helpful in resolving the problem. After expressing her amazement that someone finally asked *her* for an opinion, Molly suggested that she could barricade herself in her bed with pillows and stuffed animals. The barricade would "ward off" her night-mares and fears.

Molly's plan worked beautifully and she began sleeping in her room without nightmares. Molly concluded that counselors should rely on what the client wants to do about the problem before giving any advice. Out of the mouth of babes. . . . *Effective intervention encourages student, teacher, and parent resources to take center stage because they are the most potent factors available.*

Fortuitous Events

Also included in this category are chance or fortuitous events that somehow contribute to problem resolution. Consider the case of Michael, a first-grader referred by his mother and teacher to improve classroom behavior. The problems involved a classmate named Dwayne. Intervention focused on helping Michael to "resist the temptation" to respond to Dwayne's teasing. Some positive changes occurred, but paled in comparison to the changes that followed a fortuitous event.

Michael and Dwayne saw each other riding bikes in the neighborhood and decided to ride together. They did the same thing the next day. Within a week, they considered themselves good friends. Michael's classroom behavior improved markedly after their chance encounter. The problem-solving power of this fortuitous event cannot be denied. Success once again resulted from the student's contribution to the intervention process.

The Crust: Relationship Factors

Relationship factors are the next most important aspect of what works. They comprise the crust or container for the filling. An effective relationship with the school practitioner contains clients comfortably while allowing their resources to take center stage, just as the crust is the structure and context that allows the filling to be appreciated.

Relationship factors account for 30% of observed change in counseling. Researchers define relationship factors as those variables found across approaches, such as empathy, warmth, acceptance, encouragement of risk taking, and so forth (Lambert, 1992). Together, these factors enable a cooperative working relationship in which clients reconceptualize their concerns and act differently to address those concerns.

In a comprehensive review of relationship variables, Patterson (1984) asserts that "there are few things . . . for which the evidence is so strong as that supporting the necessity, if not sufficiency, of . . . accurate empathy, respect or warmth, and therapeutic genuineness" (p. 437). Patterson, after a distinguished career studying the therapeutic relationship, concluded that outcome research undercuts the view that expertise in techniques is the critical factor in promoting change; rather, the evidence indicates that the practitioner's influence lies in providing the conditions under which the client engages in change (Patterson, 1989).

We know where our effectiveness comes from. Let us not be convinced otherwise by clever marketing. One recent ad boasts, "Its success rate is unbelievable . . . anywhere from 80–97% . . . far superior to traditional techniques in that the client receives amelioration of the problem in minutes rather than days, weeks, or months." It is hard not to be tempted by such guerrilla marketing gimmicks. They capitalize on our desire for effectiveness.

Research demonstrates that client perceptions of the relationship are the *most* consistent predictor of improvement (Gurman, 1977; Horowitz, Marmar, Weiss, DeWitt, & Rosenbaum, 1984; Lafferty, Beutler, & Crago, 1989). Clients repeatedly attribute their success to personal qualities of the practitioner. These qualities bear a striking resemblance to each other across studies. The quality of the relationship is a central contributor to progress. Its significance transcends our cherished theories and favorite techniques.

The implication here can hardly be overstated. *If we want intervention to work, then we'd better be quite attentive to what the client thinks about us, about the relationship, and about the intervention process itself.*

The Alliance

More recently, relationship factors have been studied in terms of the *alliance*. The alliance emphasizes *collaboration* in achieving the goals of intervention (Marmar, Horowitz, Weiss, & Marziali, 1986). Research on the power of the alliance reflects over 1,000 studies (Orlinsky, Grawe, & Parks, 1994).

The conclusions of this large body of research are highlighted in a study by Bachelor (1991). She found that clients' perceptions of the alliance yielded stronger predictions of success than practitioners' perceptions. From the client's view, the most salient factors in producing positive outcomes are *counselor-provided warmth, help, caring, emotional involvement, and efforts to explore relevant material.*

In their massive review of the process–outcome literature, Orlinsky et al. (1994) conclude:

> The quality of the patient's [*sic*] participation . . . stands out as the most important determinant of outcome. . . . The therapist contribution toward helping the patient achieve a favorable outcome is made mainly through empathic, affirmative, collaborative, and self-congruent engagement with the patient. . . . These consistent process–outcome relations, based on literally hundreds of empirical findings, can be considered *facts* established by 40-plus years of research on psychotherapy. . . . (p. 361)

For a career researcher to call anything a "fact" is a point to take note of. The next section discusses how these facts can be applied by school practitioners.

Reliance on the Alliance

The unequivocal link between a favorable impression of the alliance and successful outcome makes a strong case for school practitioners to *accommodate intervention to the student's, parent's, and teacher's perceptions of a positive alliance. Webster's Collegiate Dictionary* (1993, p. 7) defines "accommodate" as: "(1) to make fit or suitable or congruous; (2) to bring into agreement or accord or reconcile; (3) to provide something desired, needed, or suited; (4) *a.* to make room for, *b.* to hold without crowding or inconvenience; (5) to give consideration to: allow for (as in the special interest of various groups); (6) to adapt oneself to undergo visual accommodation." Accommodation makes room for client resources, provides the conditions for change, adapts intervention to fit clients' ideas, and fosters a positive alliance.

The alliance is characterized by Bordin (1979) with three interacting elements: (1) the development of a relationship bond, (2) agreement on the goals of intervention, and (3) agreement on the tasks to achieve the goals.

Accommodating the Relationship

Accommodating the relationship means *containing* the client *comfortably*, *providing for* the client's desires, and *making* the relationship *fit* the client's expectations. The latest research indicates that you should spend less time worrying about which technique to use and more time monitoring the client's response to the relationship (Miller, Duncan, & Hubble, 1997).

It has long been debated whether or not relationship factors are necessary *and* sufficient to promote change. Many question the degree to which they are sufficient, preferring to believe in the intrinsic correctness of a particular method or theory. We believe that the client's perception of the relationship has a potent influence on change. It is the systematic enhancement of relationship effects that has long been missing, as well as a recipe for molding intervention to client resources and desires. This book provides such a recipe.

Accommodating the Client's Goals

Quite simply, the alliance can be accommodated by accepting the client's goals at face value. This promotes agreement about intervention goals because the practitioner, on an a priori basis, does not challenge the goals or recast them into a specific theory.

We spend little time developing diagnoses or theorizing about possible etiology of the problem. Rather, the process of intervention is comprised of careful listening and alliance monitoring combined with questions aimed at clarifying the goals of parents, teachers, and students. We rely on the *their* input, participation, and involvement to determine goals.

When we ask students, teachers, and parents what they want, we give credibility to their beliefs and values regarding the problem and its solution. We are conveying that intervention is to serve them.

Accommodating the Tasks of Intervention

The final aspect of the alliance is the agreement on the tasks of intervention. Tasks include techniques or points of view, topics of conversation, interview procedures, frequency of meetings, and so forth. Inviting students, teachers, and parents to help formulate tasks demonstrates our respect for their capabilities and the importance of their participation. In a working alliance, everyone perceives the tasks as germane. Recall the Bachelor (1991) study, which indicated that people want practitioners to explore relevant material. We obsessively attend to what students, parents, and teachers think is important.

What works is clearly defined by the alliance literature. *Effective intervention occurs when students, teachers, and parents experience the relationship positively and perceive intervention as relevant to their concerns.*

The Pie in the Sky: Placebo Factors

Imagine that you are visiting your mother today. It's been a tough week at school and you deserve a break. One thing that you especially enjoy is your mother's rendition of your favorite pie. You've been thinking about it all week. You have carefully watched your diet and worked out more than usual. You are really ready for this pie. The picture is so vivid that you can almost taste it. After fantasizing about the pie all the way to your mother's, you arrive almost drooling. Your mom opens the door and a wave of aroma envelops you. You walk into the kitchen and there it is, in all its glory.

Your hopes and expectations regarding the pie, its visual presentation and tantalizing aroma, together represent another ingredient of what works about intervention. Desired changes and improvements result in part from *placebo factors*, which include an expectancy of being helped, the instillation of hope, and the practitioner's credibility. Research shows that merely expecting help goes a long way to counteract demoralization, mobilize hope, and advance improvement (Frank & Frank, 1991).

Research shows that hope and expectancy give people a measurable advantage in many areas of life—in academic achievement, managing major illness, and dealing with difficult job situations (Goleman, 1991). Studies further show that fostering a positive expectation for change may actually be a prerequisite for success (Elkin et al., 1989; Murphy, Cramer, & Lillie, 1984; Snyder, Irving, & Anderson, 1991).

Putting Placebo to Work

Typically, teachers and parents enlist our help when everything seems to be falling apart. They often feel defeated and demoralized.

The creation of hope is greatly influenced by the school practitioner's attitude during the opening moments of intervention. Pessimistic attitudes about change are likely to minimize or curtail the effect of placebo factors. An emphasis on possibilities and a belief that change will occur instills hope and a positive expectation for improvement. Creating this hopeful atmosphere is not the same as adopting a pollyannish, "every cloud has a silver lining," attitude. Rather, hopefulness results from acknowledging both the problem *and* the possibilities for a better future.

Effective intervention is enhanced by believing in students, parents, and teachers, and having faith in the process of intervention (Kottler, 1991). When we activate and mobilize expectancies for change, we allow self-fulfilling prophecy to do part of our intervention work.

Meringue: Model Factors

So far, we have examined several factors related to change. Of these, client factors contribute the most to successful intervention. We also discussed the importance of relationship and placebo factors.

We now take up model factors. *Model factors* account for 15% of what works about intervention. They refer to the theory and techniques adopted by the practitioner. Returning to the pie metaphor, model factors are represented by the pie's meringue. The meringue enhances the appearance of the pie and embellishes the taste, but cannot stand well on its own. Without the rest of the pie to give it form and substance, the meringue is nothing but fluff. In order to be effective, an intervention theory or technique must be acceptable to the student, parent, or teacher who is expected to implement it (Elliot, 1988; Elliot, Witt, Galvin, & Peterson, 1984; Kazdin, 1980). In short, model factors have little power when separated from client and relationship factors.

Another chink in the armor of practitioner allegiance to model factors is the consistent finding that no approach is better than any other with regard to positive outcome (Bergin & Lambert, 1978; Elkin et al., 1989; Luborsky, Singer, & Luborsky, 1975; Orlinsky & Howard, 1986; Sloane, Staples, Cristol, Yorkston, & Whipple, 1975; Smith, Glass, & Miller, 1980). Despite Herculean efforts, no one has succeeded in declaring any approach to be the best. There is little pleasure in acknowledging that the model one has mastered may be indistinguishable from others in terms of its outcome effects (Frank, 1976). However, we believe it is time for school practitioners to apply what works based on 40 years of research.

Implications of the Intervention Pie

The failure to find one model superior over another points to an inevitable conclusion. There are factors more important than theory/technique that account for how people change. "What works" is primarily tied to client and relationship factors. This book describes how to utilize these factors in a deliberate fashion to enhance successful intervention.

A COMMONSENSE RECIPE FOR EFFECTIVE INTERVENTION

Client factors make the most powerful contribution to change. Clients' perceptions of the alliance are superior to practitioners' perceptions in predicting success. Together, these facts support a compelling case for making students', teachers', and parents' resources and views central to the intervention process. Hence, guideline #1: *The client knows best.*

The relative insignificance of model factors highlights the fact that no one particular theory has much to say about effective intervention. Models only provide views of situations or techniques that may or may not be useful. This is *not* to suggest that theory and technique are useless. However, theory is often overapplied and its benefits overstated. Theories provide helpful lenses to be shared with clients based on the fit to the client's "frame" and prescription. We regard models as lenses to try on, each with its own characteristic style, shade, and correction.

Guided by the resources and views of students, teachers, and parents, model factors can be helpful. The selection and application of different views or techniques must follow guideline #2 of the commonsense recipe: *If at first you don't succeed, try something different.* Some case examples are provided next to illustrate the practical implications of these intervention guidelines.

Guideline #1. The Client Knows Best:
Everything I Needed to Know about Intervention
I Learned from a 10-Year-Old

In the example of Molly presented earlier, her previous counselors had attempted to bake a pie without the most essential ingredient. To illustrate that "the client knows best," consider the case of Molly in more detail. Molly was referred by her mother. Her parents were divorced. She was sleeping in her mother's bed and having trouble adjusting to a new apartment, school, and friends. After an intake interview, Molly was labeled as coming from a "dysfunctional family." Bestowed with the diagnosis of "separation anxiety disorder," she was referred to a weekly children's social skills group.

After a few weeks in the group, her mother reported that Molly was experiencing nightmares. The group counselor responded by seeing Molly individually. The following goals were established: (1) increase Molly's understanding of being in control of her behavior, (2) relieve her fears about moving and adjusting to a new school, (3) raise her self-esteem, and (4) help her return to her room to sleep.

After 6 months of concurrent group and individual intervention, there was little improvement. Molly's mother then requested a female counselor. Because Molly asked if her counselor ever felt ugly, it was surmised that Molly had low self-esteem. The new individual intervention revolved around playing a game "to see what themes came out." The counselor also wondered whether Molly was possibly a victim of sexual abuse. Her goals for Molly were to (1) explore for sexual abuse, and (2) investigate Molly's feelings about her father.

Still concerned about her daughter's lack of progress, the mother requested a psychiatric evaluation. The evaluation noted that Molly still slept in the mother's room and that somatic complaints and school avoidance remained. Imipramine was prescribed to relieve Molly's separation anxiety.

Molly, in twice-weekly treatment for over a year and now on medication, was fast becoming a candidate for placement in a school program for emotionally disabled students. Molly's mother, dedicated to her daughter's welfare and dissatisfied with the care, discontinued the medication and sought different help.

In both the group and individual interventions, the counselors neglected to ask Molly for her ideas about her predicament. Molly was assessed, her problems were categorized, and the interventions were prescribed. What she thought—her view—was considered immaterial. The explanatory labels (dysfunctional family, separation anxiety disorder) said it all.

In the first meeting with the new practitioner, Molly was asked about what she believed would be helpful for resolving the problem. Molly expressed astonishment that someone finally wanted her opinion. She then suggested that she could barricade herself in her bed with pillows and stuffed animals to "ward off" her nightmares and fears. In the second contact she reported that her plan was working.

The excerpts that follow come from the third meeting. They reflect Molly's observations about what was helpful, and not helpful, in her experiences with counselors.

Excerpt One

SCHOOL PRACTITIONER (SP): Well, how is it going?

MOLLY (M): Just fine. I'm sleeping in my own room. I've been in my own room since I've told you about it.

SP: That's great! That's wonderful! I'm impressed by that still.

M: Counselors just don't understand . . . you [the client] also have the solutions, for yourself, but they say, "Let's try this and let's try that," and they're not helping. You know, you're like, "I don't really want to do that." Your asking me what I wanted to do with my room, got me back in my room. So, what I'm saying to all psychiatrists is we have the answers, *we just need someone to help us bring them to the front of our head. It's like they're* [the solutions] *locked in an attic* or something. It's a lot better when you ask a person what they want to do and they usually tell you what they think would help, but didn't know if it was going to help and didn't want to try.

Commentary. In her own quaint, 10-year-old fashion, Molly explains how the expert models of her previous helpers missed the mark. Simply put, the models were unnecessary for her improvement and actually prolonged her stay in counseling. She maintains that it is better to ask clients for their opinions about their problem situations.

Molly now speaks about what it was like for her to find her own solution to the sleeping problem.

Excerpt Two

M: I feel a lot better now that I came up with the solution to sleep in my own room, and I did it and I'm proud of myself. And, I couldn't be proud of myself if you told me, "How about if you barricade yourself in with pillows? Maybe that'll work." I wouldn't feel like I've done it, so basically what I'm saying is, *you don't get as much joy out of doing something when somebody told you to do it, you want to be proud of it.*

Commentary. Molly derived her own solution and it enhanced her self-esteem. When provided the opportunity, Molly revealed her inventiveness. When given the space, her resources became apparent. Her "pillow barricade" worked and she continued to sleep in her room without nightmares. Her other complaints also resolved in short order.

In Molly's case, as soon as her resources and ideas were allowed central consideration, when she was approached as a competent partner by inviting her solutions, her sleep disturbance ended. We present her situation neither to condemn the previous helpers, to suggest we hold magical solutions, nor to imply that all cases will be similar. Instead, we see her story as a good example of our "the client knows best" guideline.

Consider Molly's next statements in light of findings about the alliance. In this passage, she comments on having her ideas neglected. Once asked about her convictions, it is as though a long-closed gate has opened.

Excerpt Three

M: My other counselors never asked me what I wanted to work on. They asked me questions about the subjects that I don't really want to answer. Shouldn't I be telling you [counselor] what I think about this?

SP: (*Laughs.*)

M: I mean, you're not here to tell me my life or anything. I should come in and tell the person, "This is what's happening with this situation," and they're [the counselors] saying, "Your mom tells me you're doing such and such a thing," and then there's more stuff and like, "When did I start having problems with that?" And you come in there to talk to a person, to get them [problems] out of your system and get them worked on. Instead of she [the counselor] telling or he telling you what he thinks has happened; "Your dad's doing this, your grandfather's doing this." It's not really helping because you're sitting there going, "Uh-huh, uh-huh," and that's why I usually dreaded going to therapy. It never worked, it never helped. She [the counselor] sat down, and she starts talking. I'm sitting there going (*demonstrates her posture, looking down*). She talked the whole hour and I barely got a sentence in!

SP: Certainly that wasn't very helpful to your concerns, your sleeping in your own room . . .

M: She ignored me being in Mom's room. . . . And it is like they [counselors] think they are some all-mighty power or something. (*Both laugh.*)

SP: That drives me nuts when they think they are the all-mighty word about things.

M: Like they are God.

SP: Right (*laughing*). Oh, that is music to my ears, Molly. You know, we think a lot alike.

M: It's like, hang on, *I am also somebody* [italics added]. And you laugh at what I mean to be funny and back at my old therapist whenever I said something, well, I tried to say something about a subject, she gets busted up. It's like, *hey, I have an opinion too!*

SP: She did not take you seriously . . .

M: No!

Commentary. Molly makes it clear she felt discounted and ignored. What she perceived as important and what she valued were not solicited. Given the significance of her perceptions of the relationship and the quality of her participation, it is not difficult to see why Molly did not have a successful experience. Based on her apparent lack of agreement regarding counseling goals and tasks, the alliance literature would predict her negative outcome.

If Molly's last comments were reported at a traditional case conference, there is a high probability she would be called resistant or oppositional. In reviewing the above transcripted dialogue, recall that this is the same child placed in a social skills group, diagnosed with separation anxiety disorder, and treated individually for over a year! We say this not to criticize her previous counselors, but rather to emphasize how our chosen models can blind us to the client's inherent resources.

Returning to Molly one final time, she explains how *not* securing her input missed the mark.

Excerpt Four

SP: I knew you'd seen other therapists about not being able to sleep in your room, but yet . . .

M: It didn't help. I didn't want to do it. They weren't my ideas and they didn't seem right. Well, like, my other counselor said, "Let's try this for 5 minutes, then go for 10 minutes, then 15, then go for the whole night." I did it once and I decided, "This isn't helping!" I did it for 5 minutes and neglected to do it for 10, and then I didn't do it for 15, and then I didn't do it for half an hour. I didn't want to do that thing, so I basically ignored it . . .

Commentary. What we learned here is that when Molly tried to comply, the process stalled. The ideas were not her own. Being told what to do certainly did not motivate her to do something for herself.

Molly had become a veteran of failed intervention and the struggle for change at the ripe old age of 10. Accordingly, the current practitioner made a deliberate effort to forge an alliance. Molly made it clear that *her* goal was to get out of her mother's room and sleep without nightmares. The practitioner accepted her goal at face value. Similarly, her proposed solution for her problem was welcomed. It worked and her pride was restored. Molly's case exemplifies the wisdom of "the client knows best."

Molly is typical of people entering helping relationships. They simultaneously hold a desire to change and a natural propensity to protect themselves if change (for worse or for better) threatens personal dignity. By respecting that "clients know best" regarding their own experiences, problems, and goals, school practitioners perform an important function. Students are permitted to keep their pride, accept help on tolerable terms, and move gracefully toward improvement.

Guideline #2. If at First You Don't Succeed, Try Something Different

This guideline emerged from the innovative researchers and clinicians at the Mental Research Institute (MRI) (Fisch, Weakland, & Segal, 1982; Watzlawick, Weakland, & Fisch, 1974). The MRI model of problem development does not include diseases, disorders, dysfunctions, or deficits.

The MRI model suggests that people's attempted solutions, the very ways they are hoping to improve problems, contribute most to the problems' persistence and escalation. Problems begin from some ordinary life difficulty, of which there are usually many in most of our lives. The difficulty may come from an unusual or chance event like the divorce of parents or an unexpected illness. Most often, though, the difficulty is associated with one of the transitions experienced in the course of living one's life and raising a family, such as a child's transition from elementary to junior high school.

Most people handle these difficulties with some discomfort, but without the distress that usually leads to seeking help. During these difficult times, people fall back on coping styles that have previously worked. Usually these methods continue to work, but sometimes they don't. For example, Mary and Phil experienced a difficulty with their 15-year-old daughter. Kathleen was achieving below her potential by receiving C's and D's. For the past 5 years, under similar circumstances, Mary and Phil had grounded Kathleen and watched over her study habits in response to poor school performance. It had always worked before, and Kathleen typically would improve her grades by the end of the following grade term—until now. They first tried grounding Kathleen from the phone, then the TV, then it was total house arrest. Nothing they tried influenced her grades; in fact, things got worse to the point that Kathleen ran away for 2 days.

A diagnostician might view Kathleen as "conduct disordered" or "oppositional disordered." Perhaps he or she would also label the parents or family. In contrast, the MRI would view this circumstance as a problem that grew from a difficulty arising from a normal developmental transition, namely Kathleen's transition from childhood to adolescence. Mary and Phil applied solutions that they had previously used with success. They continued to apply what had worked when Kathleen was a child even though they knew it wasn't working with Kathleen the adolescent.

For such a difficulty to turn into a problem, only two conditions need to occur: (1) the difficulty is mishandled (i.e., the solution attempts don't work), and (2) when the difficulty is not resolved, more of the same solution is applied. Then the original difficulty will be worsened, by a vicious-cycle process, into a problem whose size and nature bear little resemblance to the original difficulty. Kathleen's "running away problem" had little apparent similarity to the original difficulty with grades.

Problems, then, often develop from chance or transitional circumstances encountered by individuals and families evolving through the life cycle. Based on their assumptions about the problem or how to solve it, people usually try variations of the same solution over and over again. We have frequently witnessed this type of pattern in our work with school problems. This occurs despite the best intentions of students, parents, and teachers, and despite the fact that the solution attempts are recognized as not helping. *The solution, in essence, is the problem* (Watzlawick et al., 1974).

The Nine-Dot Problem

To illustrate how it is easy to get stuck in one solution pattern, consider the following puzzle. The nine dots in the puzzle can be connected using only four straight lines, drawn without taking your pencil off the paper. If you have not seen this puzzle before, take a few minutes to try to solve it.

●   ●   ●

●   ●   ●

●   ●   ●

Now look at the solution below. In trying to solve the puzzle, few people think of extending the straight lines beyond the dots, even though nothing in the instructions prohibits doing so. Most people, in effect, superimpose an imaginary square on the dots, which precludes solution. By acting on the erroneous assumption that the lines cannot extend beyond the dots, you guarantee two things: frustration and failure. These are the identical outcomes that teachers, parents, and students face when they are stuck in an attempt to resolve a school problem.

It is interesting to note that although you may have recognized after just one trial that a solution to the puzzle was impossible, you probably continued to apply the same solution theme over and over again. You may have varied the speed with which you attempted your solution, the frequency of your attempts, and the intensity of your effort, but your solutions based on the restrictions inherent in the superimposed imaginary square were doomed to failure. Being freed from the constraints of the imaginary square shifts the focus, expands the problem-solving options, and makes the solution immediately obvious. New solution opportunities occur as we discard the blinders of certain assumptions.

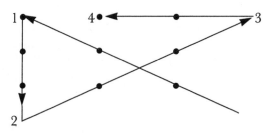

We all enter ambiguous situations with beliefs and assumptions about how things "should" be and about what rules apply. Until we get our bearings in an unfamiliar situation, we feel confused and uncomfortable. The way in which we begin to make sense out of a new situation is by drawing on past learning and experience that we believe to be relevant and sensible. This information can come from our own similar experiences or what we have learned from friends, family, books, television, and so forth. Unfortunately, when we choose ideas and concepts that don't fit the new situation, or make assumptions that aren't accurate, we tend to stick with those ideas and assumptions in spite of evidence that they aren't helping. Too quickly we get locked into one way of looking at a situation, and (1) lose sight of the fact that there are other ways of looking at it (some of which may be more helpful) and (2) become blind to the fact that our assumptions are just that: assumptions or guesses about how things are, *not* absolute truths or facts.

One may also apply this view to what doesn't work in intervention. Students, teachers, and parents consult school practitioners because they are distressed or displeased about a particular situation. The practitioner conceptualizes the problem and then intervenes. Upon failure of the intervention, the practitioner may try variations of the strategy over and over again. The practitioner may believe he or she is trying different things, but in reality is operating from a viewpoint that leads in only one solution direction—more of the same. The intervention, in essence, becomes the problem.

Like Phil and Mary's variations on grounding with Kathleen, and our ineffective solutions to the nine-dot problem, school practitioners also get stuck in repetitive unsuccessful solution attempts. Consider the case of Jamie, a 9-year-old boy referred for fighting on the bus. Jamie did not pose behavioral problems in the classroom and received average grades. Jamie saw the school counselor, who determined that Jamie had self-esteem issues and perhaps was having trouble adjusting to his mother's new boyfriend. The counselor recommended a self-esteem group and the removal of privileges for inappropriate bus behavior.

The problem persisted, however, and Jamie began having behavior problems in the classroom. The teacher referred him for a psychological evaluation, which determined that he had borderline attention-deficit/hyperactiviy disorder (ADHD). A trial of stimulant medication was initiated. Jamie's behavior problems continued. A team meeting was called that included the counselor, teacher, mother, psychologist, and bus driver. Every intervention was discussed and all agreed that each had merit. However, Jamie's problems persisted.

The counselor suggested that the team start over and discuss the original problem of fighting on the bus. The bus driver described the problem, noting that Jamie is at the last stop on the route. The teacher added that most of his classroom problems occurred at the end of the day. The discussion concluded with the bus driver's suggestion that she change her route so that Jamie could be dropped off first instead of last. This suggestion was implemented, and Jamie's bus problem was eliminated immediately. His other problems followed suit. The previous interventions had become an intimate part of the problem. Luckily for Jamie, the team recognized this and decided to "try something different."

CONCLUSIONS

Influenced by 4 decades of empirical investigation of the factors accounting for what works, this chapter suggested a commonsense recipe for effective intervention for school problems. As a brief refresher and preview, the following summary is offered:

1. *The client is the filling in our "intervention pie."* View students, teachers, and parents as healthy, capable, and competent. Invite their participation and recognize your dependence on them for success. Make their input central. Discuss topics that they view as relevant, or, after receiving their go-ahead, discuss topics you introduce. Accept their goals at face value. Make their goals your goals. Remember, the client knows best.

2. *We are the crust.* Ensure a positive alliance with parents, teachers, and students. Make sure they feel understood and that you fit their view of what your role should be. Be likable, friendly, and accommodating. Be flexible and allow yourself to be many things to many people.

3. *Technique is the meringue.* Consider intervention models as possibilities. Accommodate intervention to students', teachers', and parents' views of what is helpful. If at first you don't succeed, try something different.

PART 2

◆◆◆

THE BRIEF
INTERVENTION APPROACH

◆

♦♦♦

CHAPTER 3

Assessment: The First Interview

♦

It is easier to discover a deficiency in
individuals, in states, and in Providence, than
to see their real import and value.
—GEORG WILHELM FRIEDRICH HEGEL

This chapter describes and illustrates the goals and strategies of "assessment," emphasizing the all-important first interview. Interviewing is not a cold, one-directional process designed to interrogate or "size up" students for diagnostic purposes. Rather, interviewing enlists students', teachers', and parents' participation in a process of (1) exploring their world, (2) discovering possibilities for a better future, and (3) validating their experience.

This chapter presents a practical format for interviewing that seeks solutions in every contact with students, teachers, and parents. Tables of sample interview questions applicable to most situations involving school problems are provided.

EXPLORING THE CLIENT'S WORLD:
ACCOMMODATING THE CLIENT'S
FRAME OF REFERENCE

The client's world is central to all else that occurs. Exploring the client's world does not require listening with a "third ear." It does require the practitioner to remove intervention models from his or her "ears" and to pay close attention to the client, without recasting

FOCUS BOX 3.1. What's in a Word?: "Interviewing"

> A word carries far—very far—deals destruction
> through time as the bullets go flying through space.
> —JOSEPH CONRAD

These focus boxes challenge the use of certain traditional words and offer alternatives that more accurately describe the intervention process. It is not our intent to create straw adversaries or develop a self-promotional new language. Rather, we seek to reflect the actual factors that contribute to change in the words that we choose to explain what we do. We also want to convey the importance of language and its power to promote, or inhibit, change.

Both "assessment" and "interviewing" imply something done to clients rather than with them; the terms connote an expert gathering information for evaluative purposes (e.g., diagnostic or mental status interview). Consequently, both provide an inaccurate description *if* intervention intends to be nonjudgmental and collaborative, and to encourage maximum participation by students, teachers, and parents.

"Conversation," by definition, is the oral *exchange* of sentiments, observations, opinions, or ideas (*Webster's Collegiate Dictionary*, 1993). Although this is more descriptive of our approach, we will stick to the traditional words "interviewing" and "assessment" for the sake of clarity.

everything into the sometimes narrow confines of theoretical constructs.

Exploring the client's world requires accommodating the client's frame of reference. Accommodation means that students, teachers, and parents are like welcome guests in your house of intervention. You are the gracious host ensuring that your guest is comfortable, that his or her needs and views are respected, and the visit is experienced as positive. Just as the host accommodates the guest, the practitioner accommodates intervention to the client's frame of reference.

The *client's frame of reference* is characterized by the client's (1) resources and ideas; (2) perceptions of the alliance with the practitioner; and (3) perceptions of the problem, its causes, and how intervention may best address the client's goal. We call the latter the *client's theory of change.*

Chapter 2 covered the first two aspects of the client's frame of reference, namely, client resources and client perceptions of the alliance. To summarize briefly, accommodating resources means highlighting strengths and abilities rather than deficits and liabilities. Kenny and Molly illustrate that efficient change is accomplished when the practitioner allows student resources and ideas to take center stage. Exploring resources and ideas is especially important with children because they tend to be viewed as not having any. Accommodating the alliance means ensuring the positive experience of the relationship and honoring client goals. Just as children are rarely pursued for their capabilities or insights, they are infrequently courted for a favorable impression of the alliance. Recall how inattention to Molly's view predictably resulted in intervention failure.

The Client's Theory of Change

The *client's theory of change* consists of thoughts, attitudes, and feelings about the problem; its causes; specific goals; and how these goals can be best addressed. In short, the theories of students, teachers, and parents are like any other theories in psychology; they explain the problem from etiology to treatment.

Accommodating the client's theory of change means that all activities and interventions are *made congruous* with or *suitable* to that theory, unless an *agreement* is attained regarding any intervention outside of the client's theory. Typically, the school practitioner's theory is held in a superior position to that of the student, parent, or teacher. Conversely, accommodation requires that the focus of the interview emerge from the theory of the client. We suggest allowing the client's perceptions and experiences to dictate the course of the interview.

Bonnie and Brandy

Bonnie sought help for her 9-year-old daughter, Brandy's, irritability and unhappiness, which Bonnie viewed as signs of a genetically transmitted depression. Bonnie cited her own history of depression, as well as her mother's, as evidence for Brandy's inherited depression. She stated that her efforts to comfort, reassure, and cheer her daughter were ineffective. She feared that these early signs would worsen, dooming Brandy to the bouts of depression that had characterized the two previous generations.

This very strong theory was intensely and unequivocally presented. Bonnie requested a consultation with the school practitioner at the suggestion of her psychiatrist. In her own words:

> "I'm really worried about Brandy. She's so depressed. She gets very upset when kids here at school tease her and sometimes she even takes it out on me at home. She complains about being bored all the time and mopes around all day when she can't play with one of her friends. . . . You see, I'm depressed and have been seeing a psychiatrist for 10 years and I understand that I have a chemical imbalance and will need to take antidepressants for probably the rest of my life. I've been depressed all my life and I remember being very sad as a child. My mother is also depressed and takes antidepressants. My doctor told me it was genetic and I'm sure that Brandy is just like my mother and me and probably needs to be on medication of some kind. I was hoping that she was going to be okay, chemically, you know, but the genetics were just too strong."

We will use the case of Bonnie and Brandy to illustrate exploring and accommodating the client's theory of change. We begin our discussion with the MRI's basic elements of a first interview: the nature of the problem, how the problem is being handled, and the client's minimal goals.

Nature of the Problem. The client's view of the problem lays the foundation for everything that follows. We recommend taking notes so that the *exact words* clients choose to describe the problem and their goals are recorded. Taking notes, when done in an unobtrusive way, conveys interest in, as well as the importance of, the clients' input. It is often helpful to begin by obtaining a concrete description, specifically addressing the MRI question "Who is doing what that presents a problem, to whom, and how does such behavior constitute a problem?" (Fisch et al., 1982, p. 70).

Obtaining the student's, teacher's, or parent's description of the problem requires a dogged pursuit of the details of the problematic situation. The practitioner elicits information that is clear, explicit, and in behavioral terms—that is, what each person involved in the problem is specifically saying and doing in performing the problem, rather than general statements or abstract explanations. Requesting examples is often the best way to get specific descriptions (Fisch et al., 1982).

Unless a clear statement conveying all the elements of the problem (who, what, to whom, and how) is obtained, there is not sufficient information to design an intervention. An adequate account of the problem has been obtained when the practitioner can visualize the sequences of unsuccessful solutions in which the problem is embedded (Coyne, 1986). Table 3.1 presents questions to obtain information about the problem.

How the situation constitutes a problem for a teacher, student, or parent may often seem clear—but is it really? Consider ADHD. What does it mean? What is the client really looking for from intervention? How is the ADHD a problem? Is it a behavior problem, a grade performance problem, an attitude problem, or some other problem? When uncertainty exists, which we believe is all the time, it is better for the practitioner to inquire about the "how," rather than assuming he or she really knows.

Ascertaining *how* the situation constitutes a problem helps the practitioner understand the student's, teacher's, and parent's unique experience of the problem; identifies what intervention

---

TABLE 3.1. Questions for Exploring the Nature of the Complaint

Can you describe a recent example of the problem?
If I were a fly on the wall, what would I see?
If I recorded the problem on a video camera, what would I see and hear?
How or in what ways is it a problem?
What happens first? Then what happens? Then what?
How often does it occur?
How long does it last?
Who is usually around when it happens?
What are they doing or saying?
What stops it?
How or in what ways is it a problem?

---

should address; and provides a key element of the client's theory of change.

Bonnie described the problem as Brandy's depression, which was characterized by a general negative attitude, complaining, and boredom. How such behaviors constituted a problem revealed Bonnie's more personal struggles. What troubled Bonnie the most was feeling helpless and ineffective in helping her daughter. Intervention, therefore, should accommodate Bonnie's strong desire to be helpful to her daughter.

Brandy described the problem as her mother monitoring her feelings despite her insistence that she wasn't depressed. The only problem that Brandy identified was that boys teased her at school, which she admitted happened to all the girls in her class.

Exploring Solutions and Exceptions. The next step is to ask what all the persons closely involved with the problem have been doing to resolve it. Again, this inquiry focuses on what people are doing and saying in their attempts to prevent a recurrence of the problem, or how they deal with it when it does happen.

A full appreciation of solution attempts is crucial because solutions themselves can become the problem, and therefore must often be interrupted for problem resolution. Interventions are designed from information about attempted solutions, and usually represent a shift in the opposite direction from the basic thrust of the unsuccessful attempts.

There are at least four types of solutions to be explored: those that have failed to help, those that have helped, those advised by others (including previous helpers), and those that have been considered but not implemented (Heath & Atkinson, 1989). On occasions where solutions have helped, it is useful to incorporate and build upon these successes or notable exceptions to the problem (see Chapter 4). *Discussing previous solutions, therefore, enables the practitioner to avoid what has previously failed, amplify what has already worked, and permit the client's perceptions to remain central to the process.* Questions regarding solution attempts and exceptions are presented in Table 3.2.

Discussion of prior solutions also provides an excellent way to clarify the theories of change held by students, teachers, and parents, as well as allowing the practitioner to hear the client's frank

TABLE 3.2. Questions for Exploring Solution Attempts and Exceptions to the Problem

Exploring solution attempts

What have you done about the problem?
How did each of these things work?
What have other people done, or suggested doing, about the problem?
What other things have you thought about trying?

Exploring exceptions to the problem

When does the problem not occur?
How is it different from when the problem is occurring?
Who is around? What are they saying and doing?
When is the problem less noticeable?
What things are happening at school right now that you would like to see continue?
Has anything changed for the better since you called for the meeting?
What is better since the last time we talked?
How have you managed to get to school under these circumstances?
How do your teachers and parents treat you differently when the problem is not occurring?
If your teachers or parents were here, what would they say is different about you during times when the problem is not happening?
What would your teachers and parents say needs to happen for things to stay better?

---

evaluation of previous attempts and appraisal of how change can occur.

Bonnie's solution attempts involved long discussions intended to comfort Brandy. Bonnie also went to great lengths to help her daughter not to be bored or sad. She called her daughter's friends to invite them over, invented games to play, and spent much of her time monitoring the "depression." Sometimes Bonnie took Brandy shopping when she appeared sad. Bonnie's persistent attempts to help her daughter perpetuated and exacerbated the very problem they were intended to solve.

Bonnie reported that none of her efforts were very successful, and if they were helpful, it was very short-lived. She identified no exceptions to the problem and was unenthusiastic about discussing them.

Exploring solution attempts also revealed more about Bonnie's theory of change. When asked about what others had suggested to her, Bonnie replied that everyone else, especially Brandy's teacher, had attempted to persuade her that nothing was wrong, and that Brandy was a normal 9-year-old. Of course these answers did not fit Bonnie's theory of change, and consequently were not effective. Exploring what others had suggested made it clear that Bonnie's genetic depression theory must be accommodated if intervention was to be successful.

Minimal Goals: What the Client Wants. The final component of the exploring process is a careful conversation addressing the client's goals and hopes for intervention. *What teachers, parents, and students want may be the single most important piece of information that can be obtained.* It provides a snapshot of their theories and a route to successful intervention.

This information can be overlooked, assumed, or taken for granted, *especially* with children. Intervention failure is often *caused by* the practitioner's (1) inattention to the student's desires, and/or (2) theoretical imposition or assumption of the student's goals. Successful outcome *depends* on the client's articulation of goals and the practitioner's steadfast *commitment* to working on them.

It is often helpful to encourage the student, parent, and teacher to think small (Fisch et al., 1982). A change in one aspect of a problem often leads to changes in other areas as well. Consider Mildred, a charming grandmother who was totally exasperated with her 10-year-old grandson diagnosed with ADHD. When asked what would be different when things were better, Mildred replied that Jimmy would faithfully do his homework and do what he was told. When questioned about the first step toward that goal, she said that Jimmy would eat his cereal in the morning. Therefore, intervention addressed the morning routine. Jimmy began eating his cereal *and doing his homework.*

Mildred's theory of treating ADHD included a step through good nutrition. Because it was Mildred's theory, not the practitioner's, it worked. It is the unpredictability of client methods and accomplishments that makes this work fun. Questions related to small goal formulation are presented in Table 3.3.

TABLE 3.3. Questions for Formulating Small Goals

To students

If this behavior problem was rated on a scale from 1 to 10, with 10 being no problem at all, and 1 being as bad as it gets, where are you now? What would the next higher number look like?

What will you be doing when you get to the next higher number?

What will your teachers and parents be doing?

What will you be doing differently when this is less of a problem in school?

How will things be different in school when you begin [paying closer attention during class, getting to school on time in the mornings, turning in more math homework, etc.]?

If you went to sleep tonight and a miracle occurred and ended this problem, what would be the first thing you would notice at home and school that would be different?

What do you think your teacher will begin to notice about you when things start improving?

What would convince [your teacher, parents, court case worker, other referral source(s)] that you need to come here less often or not at all?

To parents and teachers

What will you see as the first small sign that things are getting better with your child/student in school?

[If something is already happening] What will be the next sign?

What will be an indication that things are beginning to improve?

How will you know when your child/student [is more responsible, has a better attitude, higher self-esteem, etc.]?

How will you know that your child/student doesn't need counseling anymore?

Bonnie's criteria for success were explored. Several goals were discussed. When asked to prioritize her goals, Bonnie identified seeing Brandy smile more often as very important. The practitioner asked Bonnie specifically what she wanted from the consultation. In the first interview, she said, "I need for you to verify what my psychiatrist has told me and what I already know in my heart, that Brandy is depressed like me and my mother." Bonnie wanted to see Brandy smile, wanted verification of her genetic theory, and wanted suggestions about how she could help her daughter. Brandy wanted her mom to get off her back and stop asking her whether she was depressed.

Exploring the clients' world elicited the following from the interview with Bonnie and Brandy.

Nature of the problem

Who: Brandy.

What: Genetic depression, negative attitude, and sadness.

To whom: Bonnie.

How: Complaining and boredom, as well as Bonnie's feelings of helplessness.

Exceptions: Bonnie did not identify any of note and was unenthusiastic about pursuing exceptions, perhaps because this contradicted her view of the genetic depression.

Solution attempts: (1) Lecturing, (2) cheerleading, (3) monitoring, (4) trying to fix or help (e.g., calling friends, shopping), and (5) others' solutions revolved around suggesting that nothing was wrong.

Client's minimal goals: To observe Brandy smiling more. Other goals included verification of the genetic depression theory and suggestions about how to help Brandy.

Client's theory of change: Brandy was genetically disposed to depression, just as were Bonnie and her mother.

DISCOVERING POSSIBILITIES

The questions school practitioners ask powerfully determine the direction and success of the interview. Because we are not out to promote particular meanings or to distinguish between health, pathology, or other explanatory concepts, we are free to explore a variety of ideas. Some ideas grow into relevant discussion, while others fade away as it becomes apparent they are not helpful.

An important objective of interviewing is to discover possibilities (exceptions, solutions, or conclusions) that (1) permit a course of action to address the problem; or (2) through redefinition, render the problem as no longer a problem.

Exceptions and Solutions

The discovery of possibilities often emerges from exploration of exceptions and solution attempts. Questions based on exceptions and solutions often lead to different viewpoints or new directions. Such questions empower students, teachers, and parents to utilize their knowledge and skills.

Eileen and Max

Eileen was a 41-year-old single parent who expressed exasperation about her 17-year-old son, Max's, pot smoking. Investigating Eileen's solution attempts revealed that she had tried a variety of things, including lectures, groundings, and education at a chemical dependency unit. These attempts did not influence Max's regular, though not debilitating, pot use. The counselor asked if Eileen was considering any other solutions that she had not yet implemented. Eileen replied that she was thinking of requiring a clean urine test before allowing Max to participate in his favorite pastime of sailing. The practitioner asked other questions to unfold and expand her ideas about solving Max's pot abuse. Eileen said that she had been pushed around for too long by Max. She knew now that feeling guilty about her affair and broken marriage just distracted her from taking a stand and doing what needed to be done with Max. The interview was the only face-to-face meeting. Two brief phone contacts indicated that Eileen applied her solution and Max stopped smoking pot.

The questions about her ideas highlighted Eileen's creativity and determination to address Max's pot smoking. The discovered path led to an unfolding of self-empowering comments by Eileen and a clear solution to her problem.

Discovering New Meanings

A major support for the significance of the interview process comes from the experimental literature regarding memory. Memory can no longer be thought of as an archival system of specific memories. Instead, memories are continually reinterpreted during the course of remembering (Rosenfield, 1988).

When students, teachers, and parents discuss a school problem, they are not simply describing absolute facts. Instead, they are re-interpreting the problem each time they discuss it. This creates the possibility for alternative ways of viewing the problem. A new connection or meaning may be discovered that permits a course of action or renders the problem as no longer a problem. Strategies for offering alternative perspectives, or "re-viewing" the problem, are examined in Chapter 5.

Leslie

At the age of 16, Leslie had seen four different counselors. She was a sexual abuse survivor and displayed remarkable resilience. Leslie wanted to talk to the practitioner because she didn't trust boys. She believed her trust problem to be a character flaw.

Exploration of Leslie's trust problem permitted an opportunity for her to develop different meanings and conclusions. She shared a summary of her abusive history, which began at age 6 with her father, and occurred with uncles, cousins, and neighbors throughout her childhood. Almost every man in her life, especially those who "loved" her and/or should have been trustworthy, abused her.

Each time Leslie recounted one of her many abusive experiences, her view of the trust problem as a personal flaw lost its credibility as other explanations became more plausible. One of those explanations was that she had good reason to be openly skeptical with boys. Her experience clearly demonstrated that many men were not worthy of her trust, especially those who wanted to be close to her.

As the interview unfolded, Leslie began questioning whether she actually had a trust problem. The benefits of her skepticism became apparent. Being cautious helped her to not commit too fast with boys and to take care of herself. Leslie concluded that the trust *issue* (not problem) was something to evaluate continually to make sure she wasn't closing herself off to relationships. The new meaning of her experience unfolded and expanded until ultimately she concluded that she did not have a "problem." The fact that this conclusion was reached in one meeting highlights the interventive focus of interviewing and the potential for rapid change in every contact with students, teachers, and parents.

VALIDATING THE CLIENT

Interviewing has been discussed in terms of exploring and discovering possibilities for change. The interview also validates the student's, teacher's, and parent's experience of the problem. Validation requires the school practitioner to (1) legitimize the client's concerns, (2) highlight the importance of the client's struggle with the problem, and (3) believe in the client and his or her abilities to resolve the problem.

Validation begins simply by listening and allowing students, teachers, and parents to tell their stories. The telling of the story is itself a powerful validation when told to an empathic and accepting listener. People hear their own voices and find validation in doing so (Parry, 1991). Validation continues when the client's thoughts, feelings, and behaviors are accepted, believed, and considered completely justified. We genuinely believe that people do the best they can under difficult circumstances.

Validation sometimes includes respecting the validity of unusual ideas and behaviors. Validation does not constrain you to believe the client's story as the only possible explanation of the situation, but it does require that you not discount it. No attempt is made to argue away anyone's reality or label it as crazy. It is taken at face value.

Validation of even bizarre perspectives opens the door for new ideas and directions. Validation of the existing frame of reference allows flexibility of that frame of reference. After realizing that there is no need to defend or argue the validity of a position, clients often let go of the aspects of their beliefs that are not helpful. *Validation allows people comfort and space to find face-saving ways out of their dilemmas, and it allows students, parents, and teachers the support and freedom to risk new perspectives and behaviors.*

Clients like Bonnie offer special challenges regarding validation. As Bonnie related her experiences with Brandy to a caring and empathic listener, she relaxed and shared her fears about her daughter having to be on medication. The practitioner accepted her views and legitimized her understandable distress. Validation of Bonnie's belief that Brandy was genetically depressed helped her address what she could do differently to tackle Brandy's depression.

Others' descriptions of Brandy's problems were perceived by Bonnie as minimizing their seriousness, as discounting her significant concerns, and as indictments of her parenting. The practitioner accepted Bonnie's view of her daughter's genetic depression at face value and legitimized that view in the intervention process.

Bonnie's responses were considered understandable and appropriate, and as reflective of her obvious love and concern for Brandy. The rest of the story of Bonnie and Brandy is presented in Chapter 5.

INTERVIEWING FAMILIES

Solely by bringing additional persons into consultation, family intervention offers both special challenges and multiple opportunities for change. The dramatic intensity with which families may present, the occasional polarization of views, and the challenge of validating these views can be a humbling experience.

It is first necessary to decide *who* will be interviewed. Because all persons attempting to solve the problem can help by doing something different, there are no rigid guidelines that govern who must be seen. For example, it is possible for a parent or teacher to generate solutions without the child's participation. However, if more than one person is interested in resolving the problem, then intervention alternatives are multiplied.

To maximize opportunities, it is helpful to interview the family both together and separately. The interview usually starts with the entire family. If there appears to be agreement regarding what the problem is, or there is disagreement but an open flow of ideas, the interview may continue with all individuals present. However, if there is immediate disagreement that shuts down one individual, or there appears to be tension that is preventing an exchange of views, then it is better to proceed with separate interviews.

Advantages of Separate Interviews

Seeing members of a family separately has several advantages. Separate interviews allow access to an uncensored description of each individual's perspective of the problem. Each person's theory of change is accepted and enlisted in service of the intervention goals. Separate interviews afford the opportunity to discover *who* is most interested in changing *what* problem, that is, the "customer" for change (Fisch et al., 1982).

Recall Bonnie and Brandy. The practitioner worked primarily with Bonnie because she was obviously the one more interested in changing Brandy's problem. Brandy did not see that there was a problem. Often, the teacher, principal, or parent, *not* the child, is the customer.

Seeing families separately also enables the validation of each person without concern for alienating others. Validation does not require the ungenuine agreement with opposite viewpoints. Rather, it requires acceptance and legitimization of those viewpoints, given the individual's vantage point.

Finally, separate interviews permit additional interventive possibilities given that each person's experience of the problem is addressed and each person's goals are negotiated. Although families may share a goal of improving the problem, how success is defined will likely be expressed differently. Separate interviews allow for intervention in the aspect of the problem that is most important for each individual. The interventions with Bonnie and Brandy addressed Bonnie's goals and Brandy's desire for her mom to back off.

Interviewing families enables multiple opportunities for intervention. The problem may be altered by any person initiating a change (Duncan & Rock, 1991). In addition, family intervention encourages all involved to act in concert to address a problem.

David, Beth, and Adam

David, Beth, and their 16-year-old son, Adam, came to the school practitioner because of a suicide note that Adam had written. The practitioner began the interview with the family together.

David and Beth described how Adam had been distressed of late. Adam stared at the floor and did not respond to initial questions. An overall tension characterized the interview and Adam seemed unwilling to participate.

The practitioner said that he would like to talk to them separately and asked who wanted to go first. The parents volunteered. They were frightened for Adam's safety and enraged by his blatant disrespect for their authority. They wanted their son's lethality to be assessed by a professional. After thorough validation of their frustrations and fears, the practitioner brought Adam in and sent the parents out.

The practitioner asked Adam what he was feeling suicidal about. He replied, "Everything." The practitioner suggested that things must be really bad to consider killing himself as a solution. He added that people usually have to be in a lot of pain or in a terrible situation to contemplate suicide.

Gradually, Adam began talking. He was feeling suicidal because he was under a lot of pressure at school and home. At school because of football, and at home because his mother harassed him about chores and rules. On top of all that, he found out that his girlfriend was having sex with another boy. Adam was devastated by her infidelity, because she had promised he was the only boy with whom she would ever have sex.

The practitioner validated Adam's suicidal feelings given the pressures in his life and the recent discovery of his girlfriend's disloyalty. The practitioner asked Adam if he felt suicidal "all the time" and he responded that he *only* felt suicidal when at home. Pursuing this notable distinction, the practitioner queried further and Adam replied that his mother was the reason he was suicidal at home. When asked if his feelings of suicide might go away if things improved at home, Adam replied, "Yes."

The practitioner and Adam negotiated a no-suicide contract, and Adam agreed to put off killing himself and to work on the situation with his mother. He also agreed to contact the practitioner at any time he felt suicidal. Finally, Adam gave his permission to share the "contract" with his parents.

The practitioner reunited the family and shared the no-suicide contract with the parents. The parents' fears were assuaged. Validating Adam seemed to enable his agreement not only to the contract, but also to address the problem with his mother.

Separate interviews allowed Adam to share his concerns uncensored, and the practitioner to validate each person's experience without alienating anyone. The interventions utilized in this case are described in Chapter 5.

SUMMARY

This chapter described three aspects of interviewing. Exploration permits the discovery of possibilities and allows a context for the validation of students', teachers', and parents' experience. Openness and sensitivity to the rich field of unspoken and undiscovered avenues for rapid client change is the ideal characterization of the successful practitioner, which is further illustrated as we turn to the next chapters on intervention.

Again, as a brief refresher and preview, the following summary is offered:

1. The client is the hero in the "drama" of intervention.
2. Intervention is not done *to* a client.
3. The practitioner suggests, the client chooses.

CHAPTER 4

◆◆◆

Intervention I:
The Client Knows Best

◆

Until lions have their historians, tales of
hunting will always glorify the hunter.
　　　　　—AFRICAN PROVERB

To see people in terms of pathology or to see
them in terms of competence is a matter of
choice rather than of truth.
　　　　　—DURRANT AND KOWALSKI (1995, p. 108)

It seems that once people decide to talk to a practitioner they suddenly become something less than they were before. They cease
knowing their own minds, are disconnected from their feelings, have
"something" wrong with them that requires fixing, and will do their
devilish best to thwart efforts to help them. It is curious that the very
profession that makes helping a virtue has also made a cult out of
client incompetence (Miller et al., 1997). A testament to the success
of this cult of incompetence is the significant degree to which the
pathology- and deficit-based language of the recovery movement
and the *Diagnostic and Statistical Manual of Mental Disorders* (American
Psychiatric Association, 1994) have been embraced by American
popular culture (Kaminer, 1992).

　　In the same way that people seeking help are assumed to be
fragile or ineffective, practitioners are considered the heroes of the
helping encounter. Much of the writing and thinking about school

practice places the practitioner at center stage in the drama known as Intervention. Rarely are students, teachers, and parents cast in roles of the chief agents of change. Nevertheless, the research literature makes clear that *the client is actually the single, most potent contributor to positive outcome.* The quality of the client's participation, and their perception of the helper and what the helper is doing, determine whether *any* intervention will work. In fact, the total matrix of who the clients are—their strengths and resources, their social supports, and the fortuitous events that weave in and out of their lives—matters more heavily than anything practitioners might do. Clients, the research makes abundantly clear, are the true masters of change. They really do know best!

This chapter provides practical suggestions for both recognizing client factors and making them a more deliberate part of the helping process. In addition to capitalizing on the potency of client factors, the practitioner's enactment of this guideline lays the groundwork for clients' rightful ownership of desired changes. This chapter pulls together the pragmatic application of "the client knows best" and presents the "five-E method" of exploring for, discovering, and validating exceptions.

RECOGNIZING CLIENT FACTORS

School practitioners may do their best by leaving theories, models, and techniques at the consulting room door and providing the type of environment that recognizes, validates, and nurtures client factors (Duncan & Moynihan, 1994; Patterson, 1984). In the material that follows, some suggestions are given for recognizing these factors. Recommendations are also given for incorporating them into the overall intervention process. This list should not be considered comprehensive or exhaustive. Because these factors contribute to positive outcome regardless of the model being employed, it makes sense to assume that all practitioners have developed unique methods for incorporating them into the helping process. The reader may benefit most by first taking a few moments to consider how you *already* validate and nurture both client strengths and change-producing chance events.

Becoming Change-Focused

As concerned professionals, we all look forward to the time when students improve. However, when that improvement results from factors that bear no relationship to what occurs within counseling— as is always the case with client factors—there is a risk that the improvement will either be discounted or overlooked. Practitioners can compensate for this risk by becoming more change-focused.

Becoming more "change-focused" means making a concerted effort to listen for and validate change *whenever and for whatever reason it initially occurs* (Miller et al., 1997). Having a change focus stands in stark contrast to much of the prevailing theory and practice of helping. Most models focus on how students are the same rather than how they are different, better, or improved from week to week. Change is impeded when a sole emphasis on stable patterns of the problem is used to guide intervention. Such a focus may inadvertently cause school practitioners to overlook changes that occur alongside the stable patterns of problematic behavior.

The intervention process is replete with opportunities to be more change-focused, beginning, in most cases, *before* formal intervention is even initiated.

Preintervention Change

As the name implies, preintervention change takes place in the problem prior to the formal initiation of help. There is no greater example of the operation of client factors in terms of both preexisting strengths and chance events than that of preintervention change.

Researchers Howard, Kopta, Krause, and Orlinsky (1986) were the first to describe such change and estimated that approximately 15% of clients show measurable improvement *prior to* the first meeting. Subsequent research suggests that the incidence of preintervention change is much higher. For example, in an exploratory study, Weiner-Davis, de Shazer, and Gingerich (1987) surveyed 30 clients and found that two-thirds (66%) reported positive, preintervention change directly related to the problem *if* they were asked about it at the beginning of the first visit. Lawson (1994) later replicated this research with 82 clients and found that when asked, 60% reported preintervention change.

These studies clearly indicate that beneficial change can and frequently does occur prior to formal intervention. One possible explanation for this phenomenon is what statisticians recognize as regression toward the mean. Briefly, the so-called "regression effect" is the observation that the exceptional generally reverts back to the ordinary (Gravetter & Wallnau, 1992). There is a *natural* tendency for problem students to move in the direction of improvement, back toward the center of the continuum and their mean or average daily experience.

The research also suggests that preintervention change may be a positive predictor of improvement at termination. As Garfield (1994) points out, "It does appear as if the patients' [sic] subjective feeling of change may really be the *essential* variable. If one can view this as the patient's feeling better or seeing himself or herself as improving early in therapy, then this *early* state of improvement may be indicative of positive outcome at termination [italics added]" (p. 219).

School practitioners can welcome the occurrence of preintervention change in several ways. During the opening moments of a first meeting, the practitioner may simply inquire about what, if any, change students, parents, and teachers have noticed since the time they scheduled the meeting.

Once noted, subsequent dialogue explores and amplifies the description of the preintervention change. Questions are asked that add depth and detail to the episode of preintervention change (Miller & Berg, 1995). It is also helpful for the practitioner to spend a considerable amount of time exploring what, if anything, the client did that might have caused or at least helped the change to occur.

Students, teachers, and parents sometimes report such changes without being asked. Whether preintervention change is reported spontaneously by the client or follows a direct inquiry by the practitioner is of little consequence. The key implication for school practitioners is to *listen* for a change (Miller et al., 1997).

Between-Meeting Change

Client factors not only contribute to change occurring prior to intervention, but also to change that takes place once intervention is underway. The research shows, in fact, that *improvement between meetings is the rule rather than the exception.* Reuterlov, Lofgren, Nordstrom, and Ternstrom (in press) followed 175 cases and found that at the beginning of any given session, 70% of clients reported improvement.

In contrast to these encouraging results, however, most models portray change as a difficult, long-term process. Mahoney (1991) concludes that the view of change as difficult is "one of the important points of convergence across contemporary schools of thought" (p. 18). A pessimistic view of change inadvertently leads practitioners to discount or overlook between-meeting changes, especially when they are not directly attributable to the intervention process.

School practitioners can invite between-session change in several ways. They can simply listen for and amplify any references to between-session improvement. During the opening moments of the meetings, practitioners can also ask directly about what, if any, changes have occurred since the last meeting. Finally, practitioners can suggest tasks that encourage students, teachers, and parents to take note of improvements occurring between meetings.

Empowering Change for the Future

Whether change begins prior to or during the course of intervention, a crucial second step is helping clients *own* the change. Research on self-efficacy predicts that clients who attribute change to their own efforts are likely to repeat it in the future (Bandura, 1977, 1986). Other studies have found a strong correlation between the maintenance of change and the degree to which clients attribute that change to their own efforts (Lambert & Bergin, 1994).

What is important is that students, parents, and teachers view the change as resulting, at least in part, from something they did and can, therefore, do again in the future. Practitioners can influence this attribution of ownership.

The practitioner can simply be curious about the student's, teacher's, and parent's role in any changes that take place during intervention. Specifically, the practitioner can ask questions or make statements that imply and presuppose client contribution to the resulting change (Berg & Miller, 1992; Imber, Pilkonis, Harway, Klein & Rubinsky, 1982; Walter & Peller, 1992).

Drawing an analogy to the more common occurrence of assigning blame for negative behaviors, Kral (1986) advocates assigning "positive blame" to clients following improvements. Blaming clients for success is intended to enhance their perceived influence on the problem. Empowering client ownership of progress is further illustrated in Chapter 6, and exemplified in the five-E method discussed later.

Promoting Change by Recognizing Client Competencies

Becoming change-focused also requires school practitioners to recognize client competencies. Unfortunately school practice continues to be guided by the assumption that what is wrong with the people who visit helpers—whether construed in modern parlance as biochemical, neurological, intrapsychic, interpersonal, interactional, systemic, cognitive, behavioral, or whatever—is of more importance than what is right—namely, the strengths and resources, experiences and abilities, social supports, and theories of change that clients bring to the intervention process.

Practitioners cast students, teachers, and parents in their deserved roles as primary agents of change by simply listening for and being curious about their competencies. This does not mean that the practitioner ignores suffering or assumes a pollyannish, "hear no evil, see no evil" attitude, but rather that he or she listens to the whole story: the confusion *and* the clarity, the suffering *and* the endurance, the pain *and* the coping, the desperation *and* the desire (Miller et al., 1997).

School practitioners can also mind clients' contributions by incorporating resources from clients' outside world. Studies have shown that 50% of people seeking help from professionals simultaneously look to other sources as well (Bergin, 1971). Whether clients seek out a trusted friend or family member, purchase a book or tape from their local bookstore, or attend church or a self-help group, these statistics serve as a reminder of the significant contribution to change made by elements outside the formal helping relationship. These include the clients' strengths and endurance, their tendency to seek and obtain help from others, and their ability both to engage and to mobilize whatever social support networks they may have.

The school practitioner can simply listen for and then be curious about what happens in the teacher's, student's, and parent's life that is helpful. Who is helpful in their day-to-day life? How do they engage these persons in helping them? What persons, places, or things do they seek out between meetings that provide even a small measure of comfort or aid? How do they decide to make contact with a particular person or seek out a certain place or thing? What persons, places, or things have helped them in the past? What was different about those times that enabled the client to make use of those resources?

In some cases, the practitioner may wish to be even more direct by inviting someone from the client's existing social support network (e.g., parent, partner, employer, friend, etc.) to participate, or by referring the client to resources in the community (e.g., self-help groups, support lines, social clubs, etc.). The purpose is not to identify what the client *needs* but rather what they *already have* in their world that can be put to use in reaching their goals.

THE FIVE-E METHOD OF EXPLORING FOR, DISCOVERING, AND VALIDATING EXCEPTIONS

We hope the above discussion has convinced you of the importance of the client's contribution to the helping process, and that when it comes to promoting a successful outcome, the client does know best. Treating students, teachers, and parents as experts on the problem (Molly), honoring their theories of change (Bonnie), and drawing upon their experience of outside events for solutions (Michael), represents the essence of the guideline "the client knows best." There is no better example of respect for the client's expert status and solution-laden experience than the school practitioner's search for "exceptions."

An *exception* refers to a specific circumstance in which the stated problem does not occur, or occurs less often or intensely. For the sake of simplicity, it is helpful to consider the different types of changes discussed above as exceptions. The strategy of utilizing exceptions has evolved largely from the solution-focused model of de Shazer and colleagues (Berg, 1991; Berg & Miller, 1992; de Shazer, 1985, 1991).

From a pragmatic standpoint, the solution-focused model suggests that it is often more productive to increase existing successes, no matter how small, than it is to eliminate problems. As Berg (1991) states, "It is simpler for clients to repeat already successful behavior patterns than it is to try to stop or change existing symptomatic or problematic behavior" (p. 11).

Even in seemingly dismal situations, exceptions usually can be discovered. For example, the student who reportedly "disrupts class constantly" and "never does any schoolwork" has probably behaved appropriately in class at one time or another, and has completed some assignment along the way. Parents who say they have "no control" over their teenager have probably been successful in some recent situation. Once an exception is discovered, the goal is to validate the exception and help the student and others to "do more of it." The remainder of this chapter illustrates a five-phase method for utilizing exceptions in working with school problems by *eliciting, elaborating, expanding, evaluating,* and *empowering.*

Task One: Eliciting

Most people want to describe their problem in some detail during initial interviews. Prematurely forcing them into discussing exceptions may be perceived as patronizing or discounting their experience (Cade & O'Hanlon, 1993). Exception-forced intervention alienates the client and undermines the alliance. Respectful patience and validation of the client leaves room for eliciting exceptions.

It is common for persons involved in problem situations, including school practitioners, to view the problem as constant and unchanging. de Shazer (1991) states that "times when the complaint is absent are dismissed as trivial by the client or even remain completely unseen, hidden from the client's view" (p. 58). It is important to be alert to the verbal cues of exceptions. Statements such as, ". . . failing everything *except* science," ". . . has completed work *only once* this week," provide starting points for building upon what a student and others are already doing effectively.

It is usually necessary to ask specific questions to elicit information on exceptions:

> "When is the problem absent or less noticeable during the school day?"
> "What is happening at school that you want to see continue happening?"
> "What changes have occurred since making this appointment?"

If no exceptions are identified, it is also possible to elicit exceptions through the suggestion of tasks. The so-called "first-session formula tasks" (de Shazer, 1985) are designed to capitalize on the constancy of change and encourage clients to notice exceptions. Examples include the following:

> "Between now and the next time we get together, note the things in your life [or in another person, or in your relationship with so and so, or in this specific situation, etc.] that you would like to see continue."
>
> "Pay attention to the times you are able to overcome the temptation to interrupt your teacher [or whatever the problem is]."
>
> "Observe when the problem isn't occurring or is just a little better and how you are able to make it that way."

These simple tasks set the stage for the discovery of exceptions which can then be elaborated upon.

Task Two: Elaborating

Once identified, the exception is elaborated upon by inquiring about related features and circumstances. For example, a student who reportedly misbehaves in all classes except math might be asked such questions as the following:

> "In what ways is your math class/teacher different than other classes/teachers?"
>
> "Where do you sit in math class?"
>
> "How would you rate your interest in math relative to other classes?"

Questions to parents and teachers may include the following:

> "Who is around when things seem to go smoother at home?"
>
> "What do you do or say differently when you and the student are getting along better?"

Elaborating exceptions requires the practitioner to unfold the noted difference and allow the client to appreciate its significance fully.

Task Three: Expanding

Following the identification of an exception and its elaboration, the task shifts to expanding the exception (1) to other contexts, or (2) to a greater frequency. As an example of expanding to other contexts, consider the student who misbehaved in all but one class. When it was discovered that this was the only class in which she did not sit next to good friends, her other teachers changed seating arrangements with positive results.

Clients also can be encouraged to do "more of" what is already working for them. For example, a student complained of ongoing arguments with his stepfather. When asked to describe times when they got along better, he mentioned that they enjoyed talking about sports and auto mechanics. He was encouraged to initiate such a discussion shortly after arriving home from school each day. He reported immediate improvements.

Task Four: Evaluating

Evaluation of exception-based interventions is grounded primarily on client perceptions of goal attainment. Scaling techniques are simple, useful ways to assess goal attainment. A child, teacher, or parent can be asked the following question on a regular basis throughout the intervention process: "On a scale of 1 to 10 with 1 being the worst and 10 the best, how would you rate the problem right now?" Chapter 6 describes scaling questions and other evaluation methods in detail.

Task Five: Empowering

Once desired changes are made, the goal is to empower and maintain the changes. People who perceive their role in the change process as active and important are more likely to (1) assume rightful ownership for the desired changes (i.e., to experience empowerment), and (2) continue implementing the intervention on their own (Reinking, Livesay, & Kohl, 1978). Empowering and maintaining change is thoroughly addressed in Chapter 6. Table 4.1 illustrates the use of the five-E method.

TABLE 4.1. The Five-E Method of Utilizing Exceptions to the Problem

Task one: Eliciting

Practitioner listens for, and asks about, exceptions to the problem. *Examples*: "What class does the student behave best in?" "Tell me about the time that you arrived to school on time last week." "Describe a time during the last couple weeks when you told your daughter to do something, and she did it right away."

Task two: Elaborating

Practitioner explores conditions and circumstances related to the exception. *Examples*: "In what ways is your science class different than the classes you're having more problems in?" "Who wakes you up on the days when you make it to school on time?" "Who does your daughter mind better, you or your wife?"

Task three: Expanding

Practitioner encourages student, teacher, or parent to "do more of" the exception. *Examples*: "Which one of the things about science class [that the student said was helping him behave better in there] could be done in your math class?" "Because you seem to get to school on time most of the days when your brother wakes you, how possible is it for him to wake you more often?" "What's the possibility of waiting until after dinner, instead of right when she gets home in the afternoon, to talk to your daughter about how school is going?"

Task four: Evaluating

Practitioner assists student, teacher, or parent in evaluating progress by asking questions and examining relevant data. *Examples*: "On a scale of 1 to 10, with 1 being 'the worst it could be,' and 10 being 'the best it could be,' where would you rate your behavior in math class during the past week?" Practitioner and student examine school attendance records for the past month to assess student's progress on the goal of arriving to school on time. "With regard to your goal of improving the quality of school-related discussions with your daughter, would you say things are about the same, better, or worse than they were last month?"

Task five: Empowering

Practitioner assists student, teacher, or parent in empowering and maintaining progress. *Examples*: "What have you been doing differently in math class to make things so much better now than they used to be?" "What are some of the things that need to happen for you to continue getting to school on time?" "What will it take for you to continue this evening discussion plan with your daughter?"

Dottie and Jermaine

Jermaine was referred by his special education teacher, Dottie, for frequent screaming in class, minimal work completion, and aggressive behaviors. A review of the records indicated a highly problematic school and family history. Jermaine was an 8-year-old "crack baby." His mother was deceased and father was in prison. He lived with his grandmother. He was enrolled in a special education program for students with mild mental disabilities and behavioral disabilities.

The Intervention Process. Because Jermaine's teacher, Dottie, initiated the referral, she was approached first regarding her perceptions of the situation and related goals. As is most often the case with a teacher referral, the teacher is the real customer for change—the one most motivated to see change occur. Dottie was no exception. The school practitioner explored her frame of reference about Jermaine and what she thought would help. Dottie thought that everything possible had been done, and was beginning to feel hopeless and demoralized. The practitioner validated Dottie's frustration. He complimented her for all she had already done for Jermaine and for her willingness to seek help again. Dottie appreciated recognition of all her hard work, as well as her values about teaching.

The following exchange illustrates the process of *eliciting* and *elaborating* exceptions.

SCHOOL PRACTITIONER (SP): These kids are very lucky to have you. You have really done a lot. When have the problems with Jermaine been better?

DOTTIE (D): Thanks, sometimes it's real hard. . . . There was 1 week, early in the year, that was a lot better. He settled down, didn't hardly yell, stayed on task, and was not near as disruptive.

SP: What was that all about?

D: Well, his aunt was visiting his grandmother. His grandmother just doesn't seem to have any control over him. She virtually will give him anything to stop his screaming at home. We have tried so many things to involve her in making things better, but we have been unable to get her to follow through. For example, we tried to get her to make TV contingent upon our token economy here, but to no avail. Anyway, we asked Jermaine why he was getting his work done, and he said that his aunt was visiting to help his grandma out because she was sick. He said that she made him do it.

SP: That's very interesting. I wonder how she made him do it.

D: As it turned out, Jermaine's aunt brought him to school 1 day that week and I had a chance to talk to her. She said when Jermaine screamed, she "wupped" him (*laughs*). She also said she doesn't put up with any nonsense from him.

SP: It sounds like his aunt puts the fear in him.

D: Yeah, she does, but Jermaine loves her dearly. He was falling all over himself to please her and show her off that day she was here.

SP: His aunt seems to have some special influence. I was also noticing in his record that he did better last year, that referrals seemed to diminish as the year progressed. Can you make any sense of that?

D: Well, it's funny, his teacher from last year, he adores her. Whenever she visits him, he swoons and carries on like you wouldn't believe. His behavior is much less disruptive. Sometimes she has lunch with him.

SP: How is he on those days?

D: He's better. Yeah, he's better.

The discussion began with Dottie recounting all the different ways she had attempted to help Jermaine. The practitioner listened empathically and complimented Dottie's successes with the other kids in the class, whom the practitioner recognized from referrals from previous years. Dottie was an experienced and compassionate teacher who clearly was an expert at dealing with challenging students.

The practitioner allowed Dottie to describe her frustrations and validated both her competence and her exasperation. He explored for exceptions and the ensuing discussion revealed the discovery of two notable instances of improved behavior. Jermaine's behavior was influenced positively by contact with both his aunt and his former teacher. Notice how the exceptions evolved directly from Dottie's experience. Note also that the exceptions, although dramatic, were overlooked. The task now shifted to *expanding* these exceptions and amplifying their impact in Jermaine's day-to-day life.

SP: I really think you are on to something here. We know what can help, but how can we make it help more consistently?

D: I have some ideas about that (*sounding energized*). I can call his aunt and see if she can somehow become part of his daily homework routine. Maybe even if it is only by phone, it could help.

SP: That's a great idea. What about his former teacher?

D: I was thinking we could involve her in our daily token economy. I'm sure she will be willing. If Jermaine achieves green level, or essentially doesn't scream and does his work, maybe Mrs. K can visit him briefly during her study period. Perhaps also, if Jermaine maintains improvement all week, then he can have lunch with her.

SP: Sounds great. That's really a creative way to address this situation with Jermaine.

D: Thanks. This has really given me hope. Thank you very much. I felt so helpless with him.

Dottie implemented her plan and was successful at involving both Jermaine's aunt and his previous teacher. Dottie utilized existing resources within Jermaine's world outside of counseling. Jermaine's behavior and academic performance improved. The task now shifted to *empowering* the changes.

SP: Sounds like things are really going better. Now that some time has passed, how do you account for the changes?

D: I think that involving the aunt was the big thing.

SP: How were you able to pull that off?

D: Well, I just called her and expressed my frustrations and honestly pleaded with her (*laughs*) to help, given how she seemed to be able to influence Jermaine in such a positive way. The best thing to come out of it, though, is Jermaine's grandmother seems to be more involved too.

SP: How so?

D: She is signing his work and calling me more often. I am developing a good rapport with her. What a job she took on, after raising four kids on her own. You got to admire that. I was maybe giving her a bum rap.

SP: I'm really impressed how you turned this situation around, especially how you were able to persuade the aunt to monitor the homework, and also how you have made inroads with Jermaine's grandmother as well.

D: I think that Jermaine has figured out that there is no escape (*laughs*). We got him covered at all ends. His aunt also wants me to call her during the day if Jermaine is having a bad day. Guess what? I have only called one time!

Everything about this case that was successful came from what the client knew. Dottie successfully applied her noted exceptions to Jermaine's problems and made a significant impact. The practitioner explored what Dottie knew, validated her competence, and imbued the process with hope by having faith in her abilities to improve Jermaine's behavior.

Alice, Steve, and Jill

Alice and Steve sought help from the school practitioner for their 13-year-old daughter, Jill, who superficially cut her wrist after an argument with her parents about a bad grade on a test. The parents were very concerned and described Jill as an overemotional child who was very different from her two older sisters. Jill's sisters were academically successful, attractive, and quite popular. Alice and Steve were most troubled by the suicide threat, but also identified Jill's emotional outbursts as important. Steve was particularly concerned about the long-term consequences of Jill's inability to control her emotions.

The school practitioner interviewed the family together and also interviewed Jill and her parents separately to permit the explicit validation of each person's frame of reference. No exceptions were noted during the session. At the end of the first session, an exception task was suggested. The parents were asked to observe Jill closely and note the things they observed that they would like to see continue (de Shazer, 1985).

The family returned to the next meeting and responded to the question of what they had observed with a long list of positive events and attributes. Jill was perceived as more communicative, more cooperative, and able to keep her emotions in check. The practitioner responded with follow-up questions that elaborated the exceptions. For example, when Steve said that Jill was able to control her emotions, he was asked for specific examples. The following illustrates the further expansion and empowerment of these exceptions.

SCHOOL PRACTITIONER (SP): I'm amazed at all the positive things and all these changes. But frankly, I'm also quite confused. Can you fill me in on what's going on here?

ALICE (A): Well, Jill just seemed to turn around and be more cooperative—we didn't have any major fights, a couple of disagreements, but they didn't turn into any big deal.

SP: What do you attribute the turn of events to?

STEVE (S): I was surprised at all the good things that Jill does. I don't know, I guess we were just always focusing on the bad things about her—how she's not as successful or popular as her sisters.

SP: I'm sorry, I'm not understanding very well.

A: Well, we have probably been a little harsh on Jill. She's different than her sisters, and I think I've not been able to accept that until now. I was always comparing her with them and not seeing her strengths.

SP: What strengths are you referring to?

S: She's a lot more sensitive and affectionate than the other girls. She seems more concerned about people than clothes or boyfriends. She really has friends that she cares about, and who care about her. Her relationships aren't as superficial, or fickle as her sisters' appear to be. Do you know what I mean?

SP: I think I'm sort of understanding a little better, but I'm still amazed about how you were able to overcome the temptation to argue with Jill and dwell on the problems that she has been having.

S: I decided that I was going to back off and when I did, well, I found out that she can be a pretty neat kid. I also found out that I like myself better as a parent when I'm not so critical. I've been pretty down on her lately, and I guess I haven't been too pleased with myself either, the way I have dealt with her. I really love her, and I guess I see now how that's more important than anything else.

This case illustrates how an exception task can stimulate change. Alice and Steve discovered a variety of new directions. Note that Steve decided to "back off" and seemed more concerned about his relationship with his daughter, as opposed to his previous position. The practitioner never once suggested any changes in his parenting style. The changes (backing off, appreciating strengths, feeling better about self as a parent) were formed independently. Jill was no longer suicidal. She discovered that things went much better when she didn't blow up at her parents.

SUMMARY AND IMPLICATIONS

The method of utilizing exceptions, or "working with what works," is conceptually simple and pragmatic—find something that works and encourage people to do more of it. However, its application can be challenging because it requires a shift in the way we often approach school behavior problems and the people who experience them. Instead of attempting to resolve school problems by focusing mainly on what is deficient or wrong with students, parents, or teachers, the five-E method builds upon what is functional and adaptive about people and their circumstances. This shift in focus is the method's true strength.

The following are practical implications and advantages for school practitioners using the five-E method of utilizing exceptions.

1. The client-directed, competency-oriented view of people fosters a cooperative relationship between school practitioners and students, parents, and teachers.
2. The focus on exceptions and rapid change is appealing to school practitioners, who typically consider time their most limited resource.
3. The goal of small, concrete changes in any aspect of a problem is not only more realistic for school practitioners, but also expedites change.

We hope you are convinced of the utility of the first guideline for intervention. "The client knows best" reflects our competency-based, client-directed (as opposed to theory-directed), and change-focused values regarding intervention, which are pursued further in the following chapter.

CHAPTER 5

♦♦♦

Intervention II:
If at First You Don't Succeed,
Try Something Different

♦

> The more things change, the more
> they remain the same.
> —ALPHONSE KARR

Effective intervention requires the school practitioner to draw upon a wide range of possible strategies. Sole reliance on a particular approach or technique can result in a problem's escalation. To help the practitioner avoid doing more of the same and instead develop creative ways to intervene with school problems, this chapter presents multiple intervention strategies from a literature base unfamiliar to many school practitioners. Several examples illustrate each class of intervention, and guidelines are offered for selection and design.

DOING MORE OF THE SAME

Recall that, according to the MRI, for a difficulty to turn into a problem, only two conditions need be fulfilled. First, the difficulty is mishandled (the attempted solution does not work). Second, when things don't change, more of the *same* ineffective solution is applied. Over time, a vicious, downward spiraling cycle ensues, with the original difficulty growing into an impasse, immense in size and importance (Weakland, Fisch, Watzlawick, & Bodin, 1974).

School practitioners are no strangers to the problem–solution cycle. Intractability develops in situations when clients and practitioners repeatedly apply the same ineffective theory or approach to the problem. We suggest this pragmatic rule: If the theory helps clients achieve their goals, then use it; if the theory is not working, then lose it. With close to *400* contenders in the theory market, there is likely to be one out there more amicable to the client and his or her goals (Duncan, Hubble, & Miller, 1977).

To answer the challenge of doing more of the same, a "beginner's mind" is recommended (Duncan et al., 1977). Cultivating a beginner's mind means that no matter how many cases of "problem *X*" one has seen, *this case is new*. It also means that no matter how many unsuccessful interventions the problem has undergone, *this one* may be different. A beginner's mind suggests that as school practitioners we do not allow our experience to fossilize our openness to possibility.

A quick rule of thumb for keeping a beginner's mind nimble is the following: *If by the third meeting there is no progress, then it is time to do something different.* That is, it is time to *begin* anew.

This chapter presents two general classes of strategies: (1) *Do* something different, and (2) *view* something different (Cade & O'Hanlon, 1993). "Do something different" takes many forms including tasks, rituals, prescriptions, direct suggestions, and homework assignments. "View something different" encourages alternative explanations and interpretations of the problem.

DO SOMETHING DIFFERENT

In any given problem situation, there are many possible interventions that could result in improvement. Strategic and solution-oriented authors such as Haley (1987), Madanes (1981), the MRI (Watzlawick, Weakland, & Fisch, 1974), Selvini-Palazzoli (Selvini-Palazzoli, Boscolo, Cecchin, & Prata, 1978), Miller (Miller & Berg, 1994), Duncan (Duncan, Solovey, & Rusk, 1992), de Shazer (1985, 1991), O'Hanlon and Weiner-Davis (1989) have contributed to a literature rich in possibilities (also see Appendix). The problem, of course, is

FOCUS BOX 5.1. Intervention as Invention

Although "intervention" is the traditional and familiar word for school-based efforts to improve clients' lives and change problems, we don't think the word accurately captures what happens in this approach. To intervene is to come between by way of hindrance or modification (*Webster's Collegiate Dictionary*, 1993). Like "interviewing," it implies something done *to* clients rather than *with* them, and consequently, overemphasizes the contribution and technical expertise of the practitioner while minimizing the contributions and capabilities of the client. *The word "intervention" does not capture this approach's emphasis and dependence on the client's resources and ideas, nor does it convey how techniques are successful to the extent that they accomodate the client's (1) theory of change, and (2) perception of the client–practitioner relationship.*

The terms "invent" and "invention" more accurately describe what happens in our work with students, teachers, and parents. To invent is to find or discover, to produce for the first time through imagination or ingenious thinking and experimentation (*Webster's Collegiate Dictionary*, 1993). Every technique actually is used for the first time, invented by clients to fit their unique circumstances and style. Clients are the inventors; we are their assistants.

Although the term "invention" is more compatible with this approach, we will stick with the word "intervention" throughout the book for the sake of clarity and consistency. We invite you to view "intervention" as "invention" as you read the upcoming case studies in this chapter, and in your own work with students, parents, and teachers.

not a dearth of alternatives, but the lack of a method to design intervention to meet the unique characteristics and circumstances of individual clients.

In developing or selecting interventions, we keep several things in mind. First is the recognition that any intervention *depends* upon the resources of students, teachers, and parents for success. Second is our explicit acceptance of what they want and a search for options that directly address their goals. *If an intervention does not pass that acid test, then it is discarded.*

In presenting interventions, we specifically observe the client's response. Cool or lukewarm responses are taken seriously, and are not pushed. *We look for positive responses in which clients connect the idea to something that is similar in their experience, or react with a personalized application, that is, an "invention" of their own.*

Designing Intervention

Interventions presented in this section are designed with two main things in mind. First, intervention is designed to interrupt unsuccessful solution attempts, enabling the opportunity for new directions and perspectives. Interventions are also designed explicitly to validate the client's theory of change and are tangible expressions of the alliance.

Interrupting Solution Attempts

Intervention evolves from two questions: (1) What can the client do that will stop the current solution attempts? and (2) What other solutions can be suggested that run counter to the solutions currently employed? The intervention encourages parents, students, and teachers to do something different regarding the problem. Interrupting solution attempts also creates the opportunity for different, more helpful perspectives to evolve.

Pattern Interrupters. Many times the simplest way to interrupt solution attempts is to encourage the client to alter the performance of the problem in some small, but significant way. *The alteration of the problem cycle changes the patterns surrounding the problem and often leads to improvement.* There are an unlimited number of pattern interrupters, and this chapter will focus on methods that are somewhat atypical and scarce in the school intervention literature. The following list presents several possible ways to "do something different" by interrupting patterns (O'Hanlon, 1987). School-related examples are provided for each category.

1. *Changing the frequency/rate of the problem pattern.* In a situation where the parents remind a student about homework completion several times a day, suggesting that they alter the number of homework reminders from five per day to two randomly selected times per week.

2. *Changing the duration of the problem pattern.* For a student who frequently argues with her teachers, encouraging an experiment in which she changes the length of "argument time" and observes the effects of different durations on the extent to which teachers hassle her.

3. *Changing the time of the problem pattern.* In a situation where the teacher and student often argue about missing assignments upon the student's arrival to class each day, suggesting that they schedule weekly confrontations, for example, on Wednesday afternoons immediately after school.

4. *Changing the location of the problem pattern.* Encouraging a student to "do the problem behavior" in the lunchroom instead of the classroom.

5. *Changing the intensity of the problem pattern.* Encouraging a teacher to whisper reprimands to a student.

6. *Changing some other quality or circumstance of the problem pattern.* In a situation of daily parent–adolescent conflict regarding school performance and behavior, suggesting to the father that he begin incorporating Spanish into the discussions as a way of practicing his new language and "shaking things up a bit."

7. *Changing the sequence of events around the problem.* In an ongoing situation in which the teacher typically confronts a student on classroom misbehavior, and the student ends up saying, "I'm sorry, I'll try to do better," encouraging the student to "do the apology" upon arriving at the teacher's class each day.

8. *Interrupting or otherwise preventing all or part of the sequence from occurring.* In a situation of repetitive conflict between a student and his mother, encouraging the parent to say, "Wait a minute, I'll be right back," upon the first sign of an argument, then walking out the door and working in the yard or taking a drive.

9. *Adding or subtracting one or more element to or from the sequence.* For an academically capable high school student who rarely does homework and is failing several classes as a result, suggesting that she tap her book bag three times upon leaving school each day and say, "It's my choice, baby, and my choice alone."

10. *Breaking up any element of the problem into smaller elements.* Suggesting to a third-grade teacher who "constantly" reminds a student to "bring his materials" to class, that she walk up to the student, kneel down at eye level, and painstakingly review every single item that he should be bringing to class (perhaps even discussing the specific qualities or "history" of items such as the pencil, eraser, etc.).

11. *Having the problem occur separate from the problem pattern.* Having a student rehearse "daydreaming in class" while on the playground at recess, or at home in the living room.

12. *Linking the occurrence of the problem to another undesirable or avoided activity (creating an ordeal).* In a situation where the father complains of ongoing unproductive arguments with his son over school attendance, encouraging an ordeal in which the father agrees to spend 30 minutes cleaning the basement or garage upon initiating a discussion of school attendance.

All 12 categories of altering the problem cycle share a very important commonality; that is, the theme of doing something noticeably different when students, teachers, and parents are faced with situations in which they feel stuck. Problems often become predictable to the point that everyone seems to know what is going to happen before it happens. Research in cognitive psychology has demonstrated that people process information by ignoring that which is usual and customary. For attention to occur, information or patterns must be different enough to be noticed.

Students often experience variations of "the same old song" from parents and teachers in the form of lectures or interventions.

We are suggesting that school practitioners "sing a different song" instead of becoming one more voice in the "more of the same" chorus. Unpredictability creates possibilities and often leads to an entirely different way of perceiving and behaving. "Do something different" can take as many forms as the creativity of the school practitioner allows. For example, addressing a student's misbehavior in class may include the following:

1. Walking up to the student, handing him or her a penny, and walking away without explanation.
2. Encouraging and coaching the student in the correct procedure of misbehaving, because you now understand its purpose.
3. Approaching the student, pulling out a notepad, and saying calmly, "That's one," and walking away.

In the face of a student's criticism and defiance, examples include the following:

1. Thanking the student for the feedback and saying, "It really makes my day when a student has the courage to be 100% honest with me."
2. Commenting on the student's dress or voice qualities instead of the content of their statements.
3. Responding as if something entirely different has been said, and walking away without explanation.

Sometimes, a specific intervention is not immediately apparent. In these cases, the practitioner can enlist the parent's, student's, or teacher's help by asking them to observe the problem and record data about it (Duncan et al., 1992). Observation tasks represent "something different" and often interrupt ineffective solution attempts.

Another option in these cases is to (1) acknowledge that "something different" is required, and that it is unclear exactly what that could be at the time; and (2) encourage the student, parent, or teacher to "try something different" in response to the problem during the next week. We are continually amazed by the ingenuity and resourcefulness of clients when given this task.

Validating

Interventions are also designed to validate the client's theory of change. Validation provides students, teachers, and parents a way to save face while they try new solution attempts, taking different steps toward a better future.

Carrie

Consider Carrie, a 17-year-old student beginning her interviews for college, which required her to fly. She had actively avoided the topic of flying to this point in her life. Carrie left conversations, did not read articles, and changed channels when flying was the topic. She described her fears as extreme feelings of panic. She wanted to feel in control of her fears so that she could fly to her interviews. Carrie added that she believed her fears were an overreaction, given how most people fly without fear.

Interrupting Solution Attempts. Based on Carrie's avoidance, the practitioner suggested that Carrie spend at least 15 minutes, but not more than 30 minutes, considering the dangers of flying and feeling her fears intensely. The intervention (symptom prescription) was designed to interrupt the student's current solution attempts (avoidance).

Carrie returned and reported that her fears seemed more manageable. Carrie added that she talked to other people about her flying fears (for the first time) and discovered, to her surprise, that others felt afraid also. The practitioner, building on what had already worked, suggested another task. Carrie agreed to an "experiment" requiring her to observe 10 people awaiting departure at the airport, and rate their anxiety levels on a scale of 1 to 10.

Validating. The symptom prescription (asking the student to perform the problem) was also designed to validate her experience. Carrie's description of her fears contained her own invalidation of her experience. Note the incongruence between Carrie's distress and her view that it was an overreaction. The prescription was designed not only to interrupt her avoidance, but also to validate Carrie's distress as legitimate.

Carrie returned from the initial task and reported feeling more in control, and she had discussed flying fears with others. The practitioner validated the legitimacy of Carrie's fears and the significance of her discovery of others' discomfort by suggesting the airport rating task. Carrie reported surprise that 7 out of 10 people had ratings of 6 or more and she was pleased that not everyone took flying in stride as she once thought. The task also represented a continued interruption of the solution attempt of avoidance.

Carrie no longer invalidated her distress and was able to pursue improvement of her problem. Intervention also included a relaxation exercise, and counseling ended after Carrie's first successful, although very uncomfortable, flying experience.

Bonnie and Brandy Revisited

Recall from Chapter 3 the following information from the interview with Bonnie:

Nature of the problem

Who: Brandy.

What: Genetic depression, negative attitude, and sadness.

To whom: Bonnie.

How: Complaining and boredom, as well as Bonnie's feelings of helplessness.

Exceptions: Bonnie did not identify any of note and was unenthusiastic about pursuing exceptions, perhaps because this contradicted her view of the genetic depression.

Solution attempts: (1) Lecturing, (2) cheerleading, (3) monitoring, (4) trying to fix or help (e.g., calling friends, shopping), and (5) others' solutions revolved around suggesting that nothing was wrong.

Client's minimal goals: To observe Brandy smiling more. Other goals included verification of the genetic depression theory and suggestions about how to help Brandy.

Client's theory of change: Brandy was genetically disposed to depression, just as were Bonnie and her mother.

Accommodating Bonnie's theory required the practitioner to select interventions that were tailored to a genetic perspective of depression. The practitioner, relying on a popular theory of genetics and depression (the diathesis—stress paradigm), suggested that, given the familial predisposition to depression, environmental factors were critical. Perhaps Bonnie could assist Brandy in *coping with* the depression rather than fixing it.

Excerpt One

SCHOOL PRACTITIONER (SP): After spending some alone time with Brandy and viewing the tape from our first session, I have come to the conclusion that you are absolutely correct in your estimation of Brandy's problem. . . . Given her family history of depression in both her mother and her grandmother, it seems likely that she is genetically predisposed to depression.

BONNIE (B): I knew it all along, but it's nice to get confirmation. But, is there anything else I can do?

SP: Well, that's what I wanted to discuss with you today. Because she is genetically predisposed to depression, what happens in the environment is particularly important to the manifestation of the depression. While the predisposition to depression is always there, the depression may or may not be expressed, depending on what happens in her environment and how she learns to cope. For these kinds of special kids, it takes a special kind of parenting and, frankly, a special kind of committed parent. Not all parents can demonstrate the level of involvement necessary to help a depressed child. . . . You may help Brandy cope with her depression and learn how to control it by validating her concerns, boredom, and sadness when she expresses it and then after that validation, drop the conversation so that she will learn to deal with her feelings. For example, if Brandy says, "I'm bored, there's nothing to do around here; I hate it when no one is around to play," what I am suggesting that you say in return is, "Yes, it must be tough to be all alone in the house with nobody to play with." By validating her concern, she will feel understood, and the ball will essentially be back in her court for her to deal with the boredom. The hard part for parents, especially parents of depressed kids, and as I said earlier, many cannot do it, is to resist the temptation to cheer up, entertain, or otherwise coerce the kid to feel better. Of course, all this accomplishes is making the parent feel like they have done everything they could. Another way of looking at the validation procedure is to, in general, respond to "gloom and doom" comments with agreement and even with a slight exaggeration of her original complaint. For example, to the comment, "I hate school," you may respond, "School can certainly be a bummer, and the worst of it is there's so much more to go." At other times when she is not complaining, or glooming and dooming, spend those times having discussions, playing games, and going shopping. In essence, you are accepting her depression by validating it and teaching her how to cope with it by allowing her some time and space to deal with it. I'm rambling, is this making any sense?

B: Yes it is, because I'm a stroker, I'm always upbeat and positive with her . . . always telling her how smart and pretty she is and how school is fun. I guess I sort of discount her feelings and it's not helping. Is that what you are getting at?

SP: Exactly, except you are not doing anything wrong. You are doing what any parent would do faced with a depressed kid. You are trying to help her. What I am suggesting is that you "lean to" her depression, allowing it to be, encourage its expression, and enable Brandy to develop coping strategies.

B: I guess you just don't expect kids to have bad feelings and you want to protect them from any hurt. But that's impossible to do. They suffer just as we do . . . yeah, I need to allow her to be and support her feelings, even if it's negative.

SP: That's for sure. By leaning to her depression, it may enable her to express more positive feelings too, because she won't have to defend or justify her negativity.

B: When you say exaggeration, I'm thinking particularly of her critical comments about herself, how about if I exaggerate them to the point of ridiculousness? Like if she says she's ugly, I'll say, "Yeah, you're so ugly I've had to replace three broken mirrors because you looked at them," instead of trying to convince her how pretty she is.

SP: Sounds great!

Interrupting Solution Attempts. The practitioner intervened by suggesting that Bonnie help Brandy work through and learn to cope with her depression. Bonnie could facilitate the process by encouraging expression of Brandy's concerns, validating them, and even exaggerating them, rather than reacting against them (Duncan & Rock, 1991; Watzlawick et al., 1974).

Bonnie responded very positively to the suggestions. She immediately began discussing their application, gave an example, and expressed her willingness to try the different approach. Accommodating Bonnie's theory regarding Brandy's genetic depression, rather than confronting it or attempting to persuade her to change her view, was critical to Bonnie's acceptance and implementation of the intervention. Intervention was specifically designed to reverse Bonnie's solution attempts of monitoring Brandy's depression and trying to cheer her up. Directly suggesting that Bonnie withdraw her involvement from her depressed child would likely have diminished the practitioner's credibility. The teacher and others had already attempted to convince Bonnie that Brandy was a normal 9-year-old, but Bonnie did not believe it and therefore did not respond to suggestions that Brandy could be left to her own devices.

Accepting Bonnie's theory of change regarding her daughter's behavior not only provided the direction for intervention, but also enhanced the likelihood of success. After it became clear that the practitioner was not going to challenge her beliefs, Bonnie showed greater flexibility and softened her viewpoint about Brandy's genetic depression.

Validating. The "agree and exaggerate" intervention interrupted Bonnie's solution attempts of cheering and reassuring Brandy, while validating Bonnie's theory of genetic depression, that is, the diathesis–stress model. The practitioner's suggestions were inextricably related to Bonnie's perceptions of the relationship and to her theory of change. Her perceptions of the relationship and the practitioner were positive because her viewpoint was respected and her goals were directly addressed. The intervention validated Bonnie and her opinions.

Returning to the notion of "intervention" as "invention," discussed earlier in Focus Box 5.1, Bonnie "invented" the strategy to fit her unique sense of humor and her specific strengths. She "agreed and exaggerated" in her own unique way by using her imagination and experimenting with the practitioner's suggestion.

Bonnie applied her personalized adaptations of the suggestions and returned for two more meetings. She reported that her daughter seemed happier, was smiling more, and complaining less. Bonnie also said that although it was difficult for her, she was not attempting to rescue Brandy from her depression. She added that perhaps Brandy was only *mildly* predisposed to depression. She laughed as she recounted her exaggerations with Brandy. Respecting and accommodating Bonnie's theory permitted her a face-saving way to discontinue the aspects of her beliefs and actions that were not helpful.

David, Beth, and Adam Revisited

David, Beth, and Adam returned for the second meeting with the practitioner, who began by separating the generations. Adam went first. The practitioner mentioned that he hadn't heard from Adam, so he assumed that Adam wasn't thinking of killing himself. Adam replied that it wasn't a problem any more and that things had just piled up before. He explained that things were much better and that he had decided he didn't want to work it out with his mother because she "was a bitch."

Next, David and Beth described several incidents between Beth and Adam that had escalated to screaming matches. When David was away, Adam followed Beth around the house shouting obscenities. The conflict arose from Beth's attempts to get Adam to comply with household rules. She would remind him several times, threaten with consequences, and often attempt verbally to force him to comply. David and Beth grounded Adam from the telephone, TV, and finally from everything. Even though they consistently enforced the rules and consequences, the fights persisted. Adam, according to David and Beth, enjoyed the conflict and did his best to make their lives miserable, especially Beth's. They believed that Adam was extremely manipulative, irresponsible, and selfish. As a special education teacher trained in assertive discipline, Beth felt she had tried everything. She felt powerless and frustrated, and was worried that Adam was headed for disaster.

Given David and Beth's belief that they had exhausted all

forms of punishment and assertive discipline, the practitioner did not consider such options for intervention. The practitioner offered the idea of negotiation between Adam and his parents. David and Beth responded politely, but unenthusiastically. Beth said that until Adam gave her the respect she deserved, negotiation would be difficult. Given this lukewarm response, intervention options based on conflict negotiation were discarded.

Interrupting Solution Attempts. David and Beth's solution attempts were characterized by direct efforts to obtain control over Adam's behavior through coercion, exhortation, lecturing, confrontation, and punishment. The practitioner asked himself, "What will stop or run counter to their current solutions?" Two ideas emerged: "giving up power" and "constructive payback" (Duncan, 1989; Duncan & Rock, 1991; Fisch et al., 1982).

"Giving up power" requires the verbal admission of powerlessness, and entails making requests instead of demands. "Constructive payback" occurs when one surreptitiously attaches a negative consequence to the irritating behavior of another person. Constructive payback can be helpful in giving parents some feeling of power and control and enables them to impose consequences for misbehavior (Fisch et al., 1982). The avoidance of the coercive and confrontive solutions may interrupt the problem cycle by undercutting the provocative and rebellion-inducing methods that David and Beth were using.

The practitioner suggested that Beth give the following message to Adam, as a way of giving up power to gain effectiveness:

> "I have just talked to the counselor, and I realized a lot of things. You're right, I have been a bad mother. I should back off and leave you alone. I've been trying to control you and tell you what to do, and I can't. I always think I'm right and that I know what's best for you, and I don't. I am going to try my best to change, but you'll have to be patient with me. I've been this way for a long time. There will still be rules for you around the house, and consequences if you break them. But I realize it's up to you if you want to follow the rules, or put up with the consequences instead. I have finally accepted that your life is in your hands."

The practitioner also suggested that Beth make requests of Adam (not demands or threats) in the form of, "I would appreciate it if you would do the dishes. I know it's up to you and I can't make you do anything." Beth was encouraged to express the part of her that felt powerless and defeated, rather than angry, when she made such requests. Beth liked the "giving up power" suggestion and commented on how it would enable her to take control of the situation while only giving in verbally. She also liked that it required her to admit something that had been apparent for some time: she really couldn't make Adam do anything.

"Constructive payback" was introduced as a way of confusing Adam and perhaps influencing his abusiveness, and as a way of discharging Beth's anger and frustration in a productive fashion.

Excerpt One

BETH (B): We are feeling abused and taken for granted on a daily basis. He really hurts me. He makes me feel out of control. I am at my wits' end.

DAVID (D): It really makes me mad. What should we do?

SCHOOL PRACTITIONER (SP): I have an idea, but it's one that I am usually reluctant to offer, until I'm sure that two things are in the situation. The first is that the parents have to be real frustrated and even angry, because it takes a lot of effort to enact the suggestion.

B: Oh, we are . . . we both are.

D: We're beyond frustration and anger, I'm ready to strangle the kid.

SP: Good! It takes that kind of determination. Second, it is a tactic that is especially for the kid who is completely out of touch with others' feelings and is stuck in a way of perceiving the world that is thoughtless, disrespectful, and unconcerned about the effects of his behavior on others.

B: That fits him to a tee. He isn't concerned with anyone or anything else but himself.

D: Look, I'm ready to try anything. Adam definitely has to change these abusive tirades.

SP: Well, okay, I can see how your situation is one in which the tactic could apply—but I'm also hesitant to suggest this because it sounds so crazy that the benefits sometimes are hard to see. The tactic that is sometimes helpful to try is called "constructive payback" (*Beth comments that she likes the name*), and it is intended to shake Adam up and essentially turn the tables on him so that he becomes confused. He is perceiving you, Beth, in a disrespectful manner and needs to reorient his thinking. Through confusing him, he may shift the focus off of himself and onto the effects of his behavior on others. Let me stop here. Sometimes I ramble and don't make any sense.

B: I understand what you're saying (*looking intrigued*), but how do we confuse him so he will have to reorganize his thinking? (*David nods head in agreement.*)

SP: Well, this is the crazy part. Constructive payback is the method of confusion. It entails paying him back shortly after he is abusive. In other words, it means that you pay him back for inappropriate behavior—but for constructive purposes. For example, if Adam yells at you or curses you, you may accidentally over- or undercook his food or put debris in the food (*some laughter from both parents*), or you may run the vacuum while he's on the telephone. It can really be anything that you know will be an annoyance to him, and it can take whatever creative and situation-specific form you can come up with. After you have constructively paid him back and he confronts you with the evidence and inquires what in the hell is going on, it is quite important to this particular tactic to respond in a way that conveys a very humble apology and a sense of helplessness and hopelessness. In other words, things like, "I'm so sorry, I don't know what's gotten into me lately, I haven't been myself," or "I must be losing my mind, how can I make it up? I've been depressed lately, and it must be affecting my mind," "I'm sorry, I feel so stupid," or anything in that vein. Basically, the position you want to convey is that you're terribly sorry and that you're either incompetent, stupid, senile, or crazy. It is often appropriate to be disgustingly sorry and self-effacing. Remember, I warned you that it's crazy. It is best if this strategy is presented from a position that looks like weakness instead of power, as we discussed earlier regarding giving up power to gain effectiveness.

By not challenging Adam for power, you can avoid a lot of the conflict and rebelliousness that accompany more direct methods.

B: It sounds great. I can get rid of a lot of hostility this way (*laughing*).

SP: Earlier I said that constructive payback requires a good bit of anger to implement, but it also is an effective and harmless method of discharging your anger in a way that may be helpful. It may allow you to channel that anger into doing irritating things back to Adam, but in a planned way, designed to achieve a specific purpose. Finally, and judging by your laughter, you may feel the same way, it's all right to get a little secret enjoyment out of constructive payback.

Validating. "Giving up power" and "constructive payback" were designed to interrupt the problem cycle of Adam's abusiveness and David and Beth's confrontive solution attempts. The interventions were also designed to validate David and Beth's experience. The intervention validated David and Beth's desire to reestablish parental control, particularly regarding the verbal abuse of Beth. Giving up power and constructive payback validated their anger, frustration, and powerlessness.

David and Beth returned alone for the third session, because Adam had football practice. Beth couldn't wait to describe the ways she had "paid back" Adam for his abusiveness. She reported that Adam responded to powerless requests with great confusion—he often walked away shaking his head—and, more importantly, he complied with her requests more frequently than ever before. On one occasion when Beth did not allow Adam's friend to spend the night, Adam became very loud and followed Beth around the house cursing her. Beth remained calm and did not respond to Adam. Instead, she hung her head and mumbled to herself about where she had gone wrong as a parent. Beth said she was able to stay calm by thinking of how she was going to pay Adam back for the incident. The next day, Beth enacted constructive payback by "forgetting" to transfer Adam's favorite outfit to the dryer, thereby delaying him from meeting friends at the mall. But that wasn't enough. When Adam was finally ready to walk out the door, Beth stumbled and spilled a glass of milk on his shirt. Adam was immediately furious, but Beth's rapid and pitiful apologies quickly turned his anger into confusion. Adam told Beth that she was seriously "mental" and that he was worried about her.

David and Beth reported feeling much better about Adam. They spent more time together and less time discussing Adam. They reported a more cooperative and less argumentative son, and noticed a change in themselves too. In the past, they felt inadequate and began blaming each other for Adam's blow-ups. Now they felt in charge and were acting as a team creatively to handle Adam differently. The practitioner saw the family two more times. Adam maintained that he did not feel suicidal. He broke up with his girl-friend and reported that he felt good about that. Adam added that things seemed better with his mother.

VIEW SOMETHING DIFFERENT

An old saying suggests that an optimist is a person who says of a bottle that it is half full, while a pessimist laments that it is half emp-ty—yet both are describing the same bottle and the same amount of liquid. The difference lies in their different views of the same reality; neither view is more correct than the other. Both descriptions accurately account for the "facts" of the situation: a container of liquid holding 50% of its capacity.

There are multiple views or realities that accurately describe the "facts" of any given situation. When we are stuck in a problem, we generally pick a particular way of viewing the problem, and we get locked into whatever solution attempts flow from our view (recall the nine-dot problem).

Reframing the Problem

Offering different views of the problem is called "reframing." To reframe, as classically defined by the MRI, is "to change the conceptual and/or emotional setting or viewpoint in relation to which a situation is experienced and to place it in another frame that fits the facts of the same concrete situation equally well or even better, and thereby change its entire meaning" (Watzlawick et al., 1974, p. 95).

There is a wide variety of ways to reframe problems, ranging from simple relabeling (referring to depression as realistic pessimism), to positive connotation (referring to students' misbehavior as creative ways of meeting needs), to redefining (referring to adolescent rebellion as necessary steps toward individuation).

Re-Viewing the Problem

"Re-viewing" the problem goes beyond mere reframing by validating the client's experience in addition to offering different views of the problem. Because the perspectives offered are not based on practitioner adherence to any theory, we are interested in pursuing alternative views of problems rather than "correct" ones. This allows school practitioners to select and offer views from any theory that fits and validates the student's, teacher's, or parent's problem experience. One of the advantages of not being wedded to (or even dating) a specific theory is the flexibility this freedom allows.

Selecting Useful Views

Alternative views that validate client experience and offer a different perspective may be selected from two sources: (1) specific theoretical approaches, and (2) content generated by clients.

Specific Theoretical Approaches

Sometimes clients present with clearly delineated concerns. With some problems, the efficacy of a particular conceptualization or technique is well documented and may provide useful ways of addressing the problem. A specific theoretical approach may be utilized if it fits with the client's description of the problem. The practitioner's use of a specific approach may facilitate exploration of the problem and expand its context to include possible solutions.

Because no particular theoretical approach is used exclusively, any perspective is fair game, as long as it is consistent with the client's theory of change. Consider the following case.

Peg, Dan, and Sam

An intact family of three sought the school practitioner for assistance with a "school phobia" problem. Sam, the 10-year-old son, had not attended school more than 1 day a week during the prior month. With a hint of anger in her voice, Peg reported that each day she arose before the others, completed left-over chores, prepared the family's breakfast, and prepared Sam for school. She then departed for work, leaving Sam alone to wait a half hour for the bus. Within the half hour, Sam typically would phone Peg at work, complaining of nausea. Peg would return home to minister to Sam, who, on occasion, would vomit. This pattern occurred about 4 days a week, resulting in Sam's absence from school.

Excerpt One

SCHOOL PRACTITIONER (SP): There are certainly a lot of ways to look at a problem like this. Some counselors might say, and this may sound a bit crazy so please bear with me, that Sam's school phobia, his getting sick to his stomach in the morning, is a metaphorical expression of unexpressed anger between his parents.

PEG (P): *(looking interested)*What do you mean?

SP: Well, again, this is just one way of looking at this problem— that Sam's sickness in the morning, preventing him from going to school, is a metaphorical expression of Mom being sick and tired of carrying the whole load. After all, both of your jobs are equally important, yet it is always Mom who must interrupt her work routine and come home, while Dad is able to work and not be bothered. Not to mention that it is Mom who must also be responsible for keeping the house, fixing the meals, etc. In essence, then, and this may seem far-fetched, when Sam throws up, he's doing it more for Mom than for himself.

P: That's great! *(laughing for a while)* You know, I haven't told Dan about my resentment for all this.

DAN (D): What should we do?

SP: To let Sam see that he is no longer needed to express Mom's unexpressed resentment, it may be helpful for you, Dan, to help a bit more around the house—but, more importantly, it may more strongly convey the message to Sam if you are the one that he calls in the morning when he is sick. Are you willing to try that?

D: Of course, anything that will help.

SP: It also may help, Peg, if you monitor your anger and let Dan know when your load gets too heavy.

P: That sounds like a good idea.

Peg's resentment played a big role in selecting a re-view of the problem. The Madanes model (Madanes, 1981) discusses child problems as metaphorical expressions of parental difficulties and unresolved conflicts. This particular theoretical approach was utilized based on Peg's anger and the apparent inequality of responsibility. The approach was selected based on the family's description rather than the practitioner's belief in the inherent truth of the Madanes model.

The Madanes view was offered to encourage a different and more helpful perspective. This view also validated Peg's resentment about her workload. After delivering the suggestion that Sam call Dad instead of Mom, Sam replied, "I guess I won't be staying home any more." At follow-up, this was indeed the case. The case consisted of one family meeting and one brief phone contact.

Content Generated by Clients

Many alternative perspectives can be offered from content produced solely by the client. The practitioner searches for a view holding a different connotation, which leads to different actions. The viewpoint expressed by the student, teacher, or parent is neither discounted nor challenged, but rather validated and then expanded to include the possibility of a more helpful connotation.

Problems can be re-viewed in many ways. Each of the examples below "re-view" the italicized negative labels by offering positive connotations to the behavior being described:

Arguing = Sharing emotional intensity
Controlling = Structuring one's environment, protecting

Defiant = Having one's own way of doing things

Immaturity = Aggressive exploration

Impulsive = Creative spontaneity

Reclusive, withdrawn = Introspective, contemplative, taking care of oneself

Passive = Ability to accept things as they are

Rigidity = Steadfast purpose

Mark

Mark, a 16-year-old student, was referred to the school practitioner by a concerned teacher. Mark was a "chronic underachiever" who jumped at every opportunity to argue with his teachers and the vice principal in charge of discipline. The results were consistent: arguing led to detentions, in-school suspensions, and gradually longer periods of out-of-school suspensions. Mark's grades spiraled downward. Mark's parents had punished him in every conceivable way, and had continually lectured him about the ultimately self-defeating nature of his behavior. Mark's parents believed that the school officials were only doing their job and that he needed to accept their authority, like it or not.

Mark's parents and everyone else were not only continuing to do more of the same, but also were attempting to change Mark based on a particular view or belief about the problem. Their chosen view led to continued unsuccessful solution attempts.

What would usually happen is that Mark would receive a detention for some minor infraction of the rules and would attempt to protest its fairness with the teacher. Mark would then be sent to Mr. F's (vice principal) office and an argument would ensue that predictably led to suspension. Mark said he didn't care about how self-destructive he was; nothing would make him accept the unfairness of the situation and nothing would make him buckle under to the "Nazi" vice principal.

Mark's grades continued to plummet as more and more suspensions added up; he was now failing in two subjects. The school practitioner went to a conference with Mr. F, Mark's parents, and Mark. Mr. F advised the parents that the next occurrence of disrespect would result in expulsion. He also added that sometimes it takes expulsion to get to rebellious kids like Mark, because only then would he be forced to face the consequences of his disrespect for authority. Although Mr. F was only doing his job as disciplinary leader of the school, he seemed a bit too enthusiastic about the possibility of Mark's expulsion.

Mark was hostile about talking to a counselor because it was "just another attempt by the kangaroo court to make him look like the guilty one." The school practitioner accepted Mark's hostility and commiserated with his dilemma of being forced into counseling.

After two meetings, the practitioner suggested a re-view of the problem. The re-view entailed listening to Mark's views and motivations, and using that information to offer a different perspective that validated his frame of reference.

The task was to change Mark's experience of Mr. F's disciplinary actions in such a way that Mark's beliefs and motivation (hostility and defiance) would lead to different behavior. Recalling Mr. F from the meeting, the practitioner suggested the following alternative way of looking at the facts of Mark's situation:

"Mr. F is 'out to get' you either by failing you or expelling you. Mr. F was somewhat pompous during the meeting and seemed to derive some pleasure from the idea of you facing expulsion. It is almost as if it were a 'set-up' to make you an example. You will be playing right into Mr. F's hands if you persist in your present course.

"Your plight with Mr. F has become a favorite gossip topic throughout the school. Perhaps the only way for Mr. F to save face would be to expel you for questioning his authority. As long as you naively play into his hands, you will look like just another defiant teenager, not to be taken seriously, even when you are right. If you really want to make a point and demonstrate what a jerk Mr. F is, you can embarrass Mr. F by succeeding academically and pursuing your grievances in a way that would force him to take notice."

The "facts" of Mark's problem had not changed: Mark's arguments with Mr. F led to progressive disciplinary steps. Mark's contempt for Mr. F had also not changed. The interpretation of the situation was altered from courageously standing up to a jerk in authority (Mark's view) to naively playing into that jerk's plan to make him an example so that Mr. F could save face in the school (the re-view). The problem, now re-viewed using the beliefs and motivations of Mark, could lead to a different response and solution.

The practitioner repeated variations of the above, and Mark was suspended less and improved his grades to their prior level. Moreover, Mark became a constant thorn in Mr. F's side by filing petitions against school rules, writing letters to the school board, and even calling local media. Mark pushed for and eventually got a student grievance procedure implemented.

Mr. F continued to criticize strongly Mark's efforts to change the rules. Mark met the criticisms with a smile and even more resolve to show Mr. F up, which he did on many occasions.

The alternative explanation of the facts led to new solutions. The acceptance and validation of Mark's point of view about the vice principal played a key role in the success of the re-viewing strategy.

SUMMARY AND CONCLUSIONS

> Too many therapists take their clients out to a
> psychotherapeutic dinner and tell them what to order. I
> take them out to dinner and say, "You give your order."
> —MILTON ERICKSON

This chapter presented our second rule for intervention: If at first you don't succeed, try something different. The selection and design of two general classes of intervention—do something different and view something different—were discussed and illustrated. "Do something different" was described as a widely ranging class of interventions that involves the practitioner making a direct suggestion to the client. These interventions are action-oriented, interrupt the problem cycle, and validate the client's theory of change. "View something different" or "re-viewing" provides an alternative view of the problem that validates the client's experience and expands solution opportunities.

In all, techniques do for clients what a magnifying glass does for the sun. Much as the magnifying glass brings together, focuses, and concentrates the energy of light, techniques concentrate the converging forces moving toward change, and narrow them to a point in place and time, allowing them to ignite into action (Miller et al., 1997).

Like the selections at a good smorgasbord, techniques and their supporting models should be appealing, well displayed, easily accessible, and satisfying. Many possibilities for trying something different are there for the choosing. The assortment might include the familiar as well as the exotic. Should any prove unpalatable, there are ample opportunities for the consumer to try another until the right one or right combination is found (Miller et al., 1997).

Effective practitioners offer a smorgasbord of techniques and models for students, teachers, and parents to consider and choose from. What might work wonderously for one client may fall flat for another. Intervention should not be stalled or derailed just because a technique fails to work. If the method fails, the method fails. That is the only conclusion that can be drawn. Kiss it goodbye and try something different. The next method may prove to be the very one that makes a goal-related difference. Failure of a specific theory or technique is not grounds for dismissing it forever or attributing unproductive labels to clients. After all, hardly anyone who dislikes a particular selection at a smorgasbord is labeled uncooperative, oppositional, or resistant.

CHAPTER 6

✦✦✦

Evaluating and Maintaining Progress

◆

> If you don't know where you're going, you'll
> probably end up somewhere else.
> —ANONYMOUS

School practitioners are bombarded daily by urgent requests for help. They deal with one problem, only to look up and find three or four more awaiting their "immediate" attention. Heavy caseloads and time demands make it hard for practitioners to evaluate their work properly, and to help people maintain desired changes. However, failure to monitor and empower progress jeopardizes the accountability and ultimate impact of interventions *and* school practitioners.

Previous chapters on interviewing and intervention focused on specific ways of working with students, parents, and teachers to create desired changes. The creation of change in itself is not the whole story. The rest of the story unfolds in this chapter as we address two questions: (1) How can we evaluate progress in ways that are accountable and practical?; and (2) once progress is made, how can we help students, parents, and teachers maintain it?

Instead of reviewing all possible methods of evaluation and maintenance, we address only those that are practical and compatible with the brief intervention approach. Although this chapter comes after our discussion of interviewing and intervention, strategies for evaluating and maintaining progress are initiated at the outset of our work with students, parents, and teachers. Clearly stated goals established in the first interview form the bases of evaluation throughout the change process. By viewing and treating clients as the primary architects of change, their rightful ownership and maintenance of desired changes is ensured. *Evaluation and maintenance of progress are integral, ongoing aspects of the approach.*

EVALUATING PROGRESS

School practitioners readily acknowledge the importance of evaluating the effectiveness of interventions. The more pragmatic question explored in this chapter is the following: How can practitioners evaluate the effectiveness of interventions in ways that are practically, empirically, and socially valid? This question drives the following discussion.

Practical, Empirical, and Social Validity

Practical validity is perhaps the most important consideration in selecting methods for evaluating interventions. *The most elaborate and empirically rigorous evaluation measure is useless unless it can be applied by real practitioners to real problems of real people in the real world.* The following discussion includes only those strategies that meet this practical criterion.

Empirical validity is one of the two other criteria for selecting evaluation methods. Chapter 2 presented the empirical basis for honoring client opinions in developing interventions—that is, that client factors are the most crucial elements for success. The same holds true for evaluating progress. Teachers and parents are the ones who typically request help based on *their* perceptions of a problem. *Their* judgments of progress, and those of the student, are central in evaluating the effectiveness of intervention.

Social validity refers to the extent to which changes resulting from intervention are judged by clients and others as meaningful and important. In discussing the importance of social validity in evaluating the effectiveness of intervention, Wolf (1978) encouraged practitioners to consider whether or not the outcomes of intervention make a difference in the everyday life of the client. This is a crucial consideration that goes beyond the examination of other evaluation measures such as rating scales, grades, and so forth. The easiest way to assess the social validity of interventions is simply to ask students, teachers, and parents the following types of questions following desired changes in the problem: "How are things different for you at school and home now that your grades are better?"; "What kinds of things have changed for the better in your life since your son has begun attending school regularly again?; and "In what ways is school different for you as a teacher now that things have improved between you and this student?" In essence, the client's answers to variations of the question, "So what?" following changes in the problem indicates the social validity of intervention. The notion of social validity is very consistent with the client-directed nature of brief intervention. In this approach, the goals and perceptions of teachers, parents, and students drive intervention *and* evaluation, instead of occupying a backseat to the practitioner's judgment regarding goal attainment.

Methods for Evaluating Progress

This section covers the following measures of change: (1) scaling; (2) paper-and-pencil rating scales, inventories, and checklists; (3) permanent product data; and (4) single-case designs.

Scaling

The simplest way to assess change from the perspective of students, teachers, and parents is to ask them. *Scaling* assesses a person's judgment regarding the size of the problem. Students, teachers, and parents can be asked the following question throughout the intervention process: "On a scale of 1 to 10, with 1 being 'the worst it can be,' and 10 being 'the best it can be,' where would you rate the problem right now?" Scaling techniques are applicable to a broad range of people, problems, goals, and interventions. The versatility of scaling techniques makes them especially useful to school practitioners who deal with a wide range of problems and individuals. Scaling can be adapted to fit the uniqueness of clients and their goals. For example, the scale can be made more graphic and concrete for younger children by drawing a line on paper and asking (while pointing accordingly), "If this bottom part shows where you were when you used to get in trouble a lot at school, and this top part shows where you would be if things were perfect at school and you never got in trouble, point to where you would put yourself right now." Children old enough to understand number concepts respond very well to scaling, as do most adults (Berg, 1991). Scaling also works well with parents and students who are less skilled and comfortable with words. People appreciate the inherent respect shown by questions that tap *their* perceptions of progress. These questions serve to evaluate change and empower the collaborative relationship on an ongoing basis. Table 6.1 provides examples of scaling questions for evaluating progress. Refer to Durrant (1995) and Kowalski and Kral (1989) for additional discussion and examples of scaling questions.

Paper-and-Pencil Methods

The use of *paper-and-pencil rating scales, inventories, and checklists* is another way of evaluating progress. A teacher or parent could evaluate a student on a behavioral rating scale prior to and following intervention. A student might complete a pre- and postintervention social skills checklist to assess a goal of "getting along better with others." Standardized rating scales may be useful for evaluating progress toward some goals. However, they will not sufficiently address most of the highly individualized goals of brief intervention. Consider the following goals developed in collaboration with students: (1) to "not get referred" for another foster home placement, (2) to earn a grade of D in English class in order to graduate, and (3) to start at least "one conversation a day with my mother" about school. Progress toward these unique, student-developed goals cannot be properly monitored with standardized rating scales. We suggest caution in selecting such measures, especially if they will serve as the sole criterion for evaluating change.

Permanent Product Data

Examination of *permanent product data* such as report cards and discipline records is another practical way to evaluate progress on school-related goals. These data can be easily incorporated into sin-

TABLE 6.1. Scaling Questions for Evaluating Progress with Students, Parents, and Teachers

Students

On a scale of 1 to 10, with 10 being exactly how you want things to be, and 1 being the worst things can be, where would you put things right now?

On a scale of 1 to 10, with 10 being "feeling very, very calm and relaxed," and 1 being "feeling really, really uptight and nervous," where would you say you were right before the big science test yesterday? How does that compare to where you were about 2 months ago before important science tests?

On a scale of 1 to 100, with 1 being "this stuff is totally boring and sucks bigtime," and 100 being "this stuff is totally cool, I can't get enough of it," where would you rate your interest in math right now?

If you were to rate your behavior in your social studies class during the past week, where this [practitioner holds hand just above the floor] is the worst it's been all year, and this [hand above head] is where it needs to be for your teacher and your parents to get off your case about it, where would you say it is now?

Look at these five blocks. One block [practitioner sets one block on the table] means you're teasing and hitting other kids, and getting in lots of trouble at school, and five blocks [practitioner lines up five blocks] means you're being real polite to other kids and keeping your hands to yourself. Could you set up these blocks to show how you're doing at school today?

Parents

On a scale of 1 to 100, with 100 being how you want things to be between you and your daughter, and 1 being the worst things could be, where would you say things were when you first called for help on this problem? Where would you put things right now?

On a scale of 1 to 10, with 10 being "as good as it gets," and 1 being "the worst it could be," where would you say things have been during the last week in terms of Michael's success in following the homework routine?

If you were to rate Camilla's progress in waking up on her own in order to get to school on time on a scale of 0 to 10, with 0 being "the pits," and 10 being, "super," where would say she was a month ago? Where would you say she was during the past week?

Teachers

On a scale of 1 to 100, with 100 being "gets along great with peers on the playground," and 1 being "doesn't get along at all," where would you say Teresa is right now? Where would she need to get to so she is no longer considered "a problem" on the playground?

On a scale of 0 to 10, with 0 being "no effort whatsoever," and 10 being "very strong effort," where would you place Kevin's effort to pay attention in class now?

With regard to your goal of using a softer voice in the classroom, where would you rate yourself right now on a scale of 1 to 10, with 10 being "total success," and 1 being "no success whatsoever"?

gle-case designs. For example, comparison of report cards and attendance records before, during, and following intervention could be used to evaluate the student's goals of earning passing grades and arriving to school on time. Additional permanent products include classroom work samples, homework assignments, midterm progress reports, teachers' gradebooks, and students' cumulative files.

Single-Case Designs

Single-case time-series designs (Barlow, Hayes, & Nelson, 1984) can be utilized with other methods to evaluate progress. The simplest of these designs is the "AB" or "reversal." The AB design involves ongoing measures of clients' performance or judgments of key target goals or behaviors prior to ("A" or "baseline" phase) and following intervention ("B" or "intervention" phase) (Kazdin, 1994). For example, a teacher might rate or "scale" a student's daily classroom behavior before, during, and following counseling. The case study in Chapter 8 provides an example in which an AB design was tailored to fit the unique circumstances and goals of the student and parents. The AB design is a simple way of monitoring progress that is particularly suitable for use in school settings (Kratochwill & Bergan, 1990). The use of single-case time-series designs is addressed in greater detail elsewhere (Barlow et al., 1984; Bergan & Kratochwill, 1990).

Final Comment on Evaluating Progress

Even under sterile and well-controlled laboratory conditions, conclusions regarding intervention effects are always subject to internal validity threats (conditions or circumstances other than the treatment itself that might have influenced measured changes). These threats are multiplied in the empirically murky waters of natural settings like schools and homes. The evaluation methods presented above are subject to many internal validity threats. We are not trying to win awards for experimental rigor or research design, but to promote accountable practices that are compatible with the client-directed focus of brief intervention. *Evaluation methods must be practical if they are to be used at all.* The ideas and techniques presented above represent an integration of the approach's major empirical and conceptual foundations into user-friendly ways of evaluating clients' progress.

MAINTAINING PROGRESS

When desired changes occur at any point in the intervention process, efforts shift toward maintaining them. Maintaining progress is often ignored or minimized in the flurry of heavy caseloads and other demands in the everyday life of school practitioners. *Maintenance strategies must be time effective and user friendly* for busy school practitioners. We suggest "beginning with the end in mind" by employing maintenance strategies *throughout* the helping process, not just at the very end. This section presents several practical methods for empowering and maintaining changes in school problems, as summarized in Table 6.2.

Collaborating

The establishment and ongoing promotion of a collaborative relationship goes a long way in helping students, parents, and teachers maintain improvements. People who perceive their role in the change process as active and significant are more likely to continue implementing successful interventions on their own (Reinking et al., 1978).

Gutkin and Curtis (1990) cite the following components of effective collaboration between school practitioners and teachers, parents, and students (whom they refer to as "consultees"): (1) consultees' active involvement in problem solving; (2) coordinate, nonhierarchical power status between school practitioners and consultees; (3) voluntary *versus* coerced participation of consultees in the problem-solving process; and (4) consultees' right to reject any interventions offered by school practitioners. The following strategies for maintaining progress are consistent with these components of effective collaboration.

A *one-down collaborative style* (Fisch et al., 1982) is more effective than an expert or authoritarian style in promoting cooperative relationships that increase clients' ownership and maintenance of de-

TABLE 6.2. Methods for Maintaining Progress

Collaborating

Practitioner collaborates versus dictates throughout the intervention process. *Examples*: "Offering suggestions" instead of "telling" people what to do ("What would you think about mailing a letter to the student instead of discussing things right after class?"); presenting interpretations and suggestions in a tentative manner ("I'm not sure about this, but I'm wondering if you actually control the teacher as much as he controls you").

"Blaming" clients for success

Practitioner blames parents, teachers, and students for desired changes. *Examples*: "How did you manage to get your son to school on time 4 out of 5 days last week?" "What are you doing different now to make it through the whole day without getting kicked out of class?"

Empowering clients' plans to maintain progress

Practitioner empowers students', teachers', and parents' ideas and plans for maintaining progress. *Examples*: "What can you do to help continue the progress you have made with this student in your math class?" "What would your parents say needs to happen for you to continue having car privileges?"

Helping clients prepare for relapse

Practitioner suggests that occasional relapses are part of the change process, and encourages clients to develop strategies for handling them. *Examples*: "What can you do if your daughter does not get up for school one day next week?" "What are some specific things you can do if you start falling behind in English class again?"

Leaving the door open

Practitioner offers follow-up meetings or phone contacts at the client's request.

---

sired changes. The phrase "one-down" is used to convey the practitioner's collaborative status with the client, as compared to the traditional expert approach in which the practitioner's opinions and ideas are presented as superior, or "one-up," to those of the client. The practitioner's opinions and ideas are always secondary to those of the client in the brief intervention approach. In advocating the one-down practitioner style, Weakland and Fisch (1992, p. 316) offer the following comment: "We prefer that the client not feel she is a passive and helpless puppet fortunate enough to have encountered a master puppeteer but is an active participant in the resolution of the problem."

The one-down style is enhanced by (1) *"offering suggestions"* instead of *telling people what to do,* such as by asking, "What would you think about trying this for a week as an experiment?"; (2) *presenting interpretations and suggestions in a tentative manner* that allows the student, teacher, or parent to accept or reject them freely, such as by saying, "I don't know if this is on target or not, but I'm wondering if your teacher gets on you a lot because she really wants you to do well"; and (3) *relying on students, parents, and teachers to "educate" us* regarding their views of the problem and potential solutions, such as by saying, "It would really help me to understand your theories about what's going on here and what we might do to turn things around." Duncan et al. (1992) recommend adopting the attitude of "an alien trying to make sense of the client's world" (p. 53). This "alien" perspective paves the way for students, parents, and teachers to assume greater ownership and credit for improvements, and to sustain these improvements in the future.

We are not suggesting that practitioners refrain from making suggestions or sharing their expertise with clients. Parents, teachers, and students often request suggestions from us, and we oblige. Making suggestions "by invitation only" preserves the collaborative relationship and client-directed focus of the approach. A collaborative relationship helps to ensure students', teachers', and parents' ownership and maintenance of desired changes, regardless of who actually "comes up with" a useful idea or intervention.

"Blaming" Clients for Success

Viewing people as competent helps to initiate *and* sustain positive changes. Discovering and amplifying students', parents', and teachers' unique strengths and resources conveys our faith in their ability to resolve problems during and following our work with them.

People may initially view a positive change in the problem as "a fluke," assuming little or no credit for it. We *explicitly blame students, teachers, and parents for desired changes in the problem.* Change is hard work, and we acknowledge this when we ask people how they managed to do it, with questions such as, "What did you do different this time that led to a B on the math test?" Blaming clients for desired changes may enhance their sense of "self-efficacy" (Bandura, 1977) and "personal agency" (White & Epston, 1990). Students, teachers, and parents who attribute desired changes in a school problem to their personal thoughts or actions are more likely to own and maintain such changes.

Blaming the client for success is illustrated in the following conversation with Rachelle, a high school student. The school practitioner acknowledges the "hard work" of change and explores specifically *what* Rachelle did to bring it about. Rachelle was referred for counseling because she refused to participate in physical education (PE) class and was at risk for failing the class for the second year in a row. This meeting occurred following a week of successful participation in PE class.

SCHOOL PRACTITIONER (SP): Mr. Yauss [PE teacher] told me you've been dressing for PE.

RACHELLE (R): Yeah.

SP: That's great. What are you doing to make that happen?

R: I don't know, just going, I guess.

SP: Wow. That's quite a change from where things were only last week or so, isn't it?

R: Yeah.

SP: Tell me what you've done differently about this PE thing this week as compared to last week.

R: Well, I don't know. I just decided it wasn't worth getting hassled about all the time.

SP: So you didn't want to keep getting hassled.

R: Right.

SP: Still, I've met a lot of students, some even older than you, that didn't want to get hassled, but still didn't make the kind of changes you've made. They said they wanted to, but they didn't follow through with action like you did. That's hard work. How did you do that?

R: One thing is your attitude. You just gotta do it. Like the TV says, "Just do it." That's what I did. I just did it. (*Laughs.*)

SP: You sure did. You know, I ask you this stuff because I'm real interested in how you did it. Another reason I ask is because my job is to help people change things in school, and I figure, who best to ask than people who have proven they can do this? People like you. So, you can help me do my job better by giving me ideas on how you went about making this change.

R: Yeah. Well, I don't know. It's hard to think of something.

SP: If another high school student was sitting here with us and asked you for advice on how to get her act together and go to PE class, what would you tell her?

R: Okay, first I'd say, "Think about how the skipping class and stuff is affecting you. I mean, you might be having fun and stuff while you're skipping, but you probably get bored like I did, and you just kind of keep doing it 'cause you don't know no better. You're just hurting yourself because if you fail the class, you have to keep taking it over again, you can't get out of it. So you have to think about what you really want to do, 'cause your parents or even teachers can't make you do it, you've got to decide to do it yourself, 'cause if you don't, it just builds up and keeps getting worse. It don't get no better. You get further behind, and people keep hassling you, calling your mom and stuff. So, even if the class is stupid, you're better off going than messing around and wasting time.

SP: Anything else?

R: Well, if you want to graduate, you've got to go to classes and pass them. A lot of kids just fail them and have to keep repeating them. That's stupid. If you don't graduate, you'll end up with a dumb job. You won't be able to make anything out of your life.

SP: Anything else?

R: No, that's it.

SP: Wow. Thanks. That's some great advice. You could make a video for high school students who skip PE. (*Rachelle laughs.*) Great ideas. Can I steal them? I mean, can I use them with other students?

R: (*smiling*) Sure.

Students, parents, and teachers appreciate and enjoy the chance to reflect upon their success. Providing opportunities for them to clarify what they did to bring about success may help them to recall and apply such strategies in the future. Rachelle had some ups and downs in PE class throughout the remainder of the year, but the ups were sufficient to meet her goal of passing the class.

Another way to encourage parents, teachers, and students to reflect upon and take credit for desired changes is to ask how they "resisted" the urge or temptation to do things the way they used to, with questions such as, "How did you resist the temptation to cuss out the teacher like you used to?". These questions extend the notion that "change is hard work," and convey the practitioner's faith in the client's ability to "resist" old patterns in favor of new, more productive ones.

In the following meeting with a sixth grader-named Greg, the school practitioner empowers change by (1) clarifying Greg's role in bringing about the change, and (2) exploring how he resisted old habits and patterns. The meeting occurred following small but noticeable improvements in Greg's homework completion and classroom behavior. The dialogue begins following a scaling question in which Greg reported moving from a "3" to a "6" in homework completion.

SCHOOL PRACTITIONER (SP): 3 to 6. Wow. What did you do to get from 3 to 6?

GREG (G): I'm doing my homework after school. That's the main thing.

SP: Okay. That's different than before, right?

G: I used to do it, well, *when* I did it (*laughs*), sometime after supper when it got dark outside.

SP: Okay. So you've changed your homework time?

G: Yeah. Well, my mom kinda changed it for me, but I like it 'cause I get it done, then I can go out.

SP: I see. So your mom sort of helped you change your schedule. But your mom used to get on you before about homework, and you still didn't get much done, right?

G: No. I guess not.

SP: So, there's something real different about this now, what you're doing now, compared to the past, because your mom always used to ride you about homework, and you didn't do much of it. But now, you do it after school. What made you decide to do that?

G: Well, my teachers and my Mom were getting on me all the time.

SP: So they just wore you down, huh?

G: (*Laughs.*) Kind of.

SP: You didn't like that.

G: No. (*Laughs.*)

SP: Still, they can't, like, take your hand and put a pencil in it and do your homework for you, right?

G: Right.

SP: You're the only one who can do that, and you're doing it. So, somehow *you* made a change here. 'Cause it's you who's doing the homework.

G: Yeah, I guess so.

SP: Let me ask you this. When we first talked about this homework thing, you told me how hard it was to do homework when it was light outside and your friends were always out playing. Remember that?

G: Yeah.

SP: Is it still hard to stay in and do homework when it's light?

G: Yeah.

SP: So, how do you resist the temptation to just bag the homework and run out and play right after school like you used to?

G: I just decided "Hey, it ain't worth it," getting F's in spelling and math. I don't want to flunk out.

SP: It's still tempting though, right?

G: Yeah, but it ain't really worth it. Besides, I can get it done pretty quick and I still get outside about 4:30 or something. Plus I don't get yelled out.

SP: What else do you tell yourself that helps you get your homework done after school?

G: Well, I just say, "If I do this, I'll pass my classes and I won't be a stupid flunkie in sixth grade again." I don't want to be one of those kids that flunk and end up in the same grade for 3 years. (*Laughs.*)

SP: So it really was *your* decision to change this homework thing, huh?

G: Yeah.

Greg and the school practitioner continued to explore ways for him to sustain improvements by not giving in to the urge to do things the old way. His receipt of the "most improved" student award at the end of the year was testimony to his commitment and skills in maintaining improvements.

Blaming students, teachers, and parents for success helps them maintain it in the future. This strategy highlights the approach's competency orientation. Next, we present ways to explore and empower clients' plans to continue "doing what works" in the future.

Exploring and Empowering Clients' Plans to Maintain Progress

Empowering students', parents', and teachers' intentions and plans to maintain progress involves variations on the question, "What are your plans for maintaining desired changes?" This line of questioning (1) helps clients to develop and clarify plans for sustaining improvements, and (2) conveys a positive expectancy and confidence in their ability to do so. Sometimes it helps to ask students, teachers, and parents what others would say needs to happen for improvements to continue ("What do you think your teacher would say needs to happen for you to continue passing history?"). This invites different perspectives and ideas that they may not otherwise consider.

The following excerpt is taken from a meeting between the school practitioner and Angelique, a 10th-grader referred for "truancy, talking out in class, and refusing to serve detention." The meeting took place following 2 successful days at school during which she received no discipline slips. The school practitioner explores *what she did* to get herself to school and to stay out of trouble on those days, as well as her *future plans* regarding these improvements.

SCHOOL PRACTITIONER (SP): So, you set your alarm and reminded your mother to wake you if you weren't up by 7:30. Did the alarm go off?

ANGELIQUE (A): Yeah. And I got up.

SP: Whoa. That's great. I know some adults who struggle with getting up by an alarm. You know, they keep hitting the snooze button and end up late for work. What's your secret?

A: (*Laughs.*) I put it all the way across the room so I have to get up to shut it off.

SP: (*Laughs.*) What a great idea.

A: Yeah, my mom was pretty surprised.

SP: Surprised about what?

A: About me getting up on time and going to school.

SP: I'll bet. Have you ever done that before, I mean, without reminders or somebody else waking you?

A: Yeah, I did it before. But not much lately.

SP: What made you decide to do it *now?*

A: I don't want 2 years of detention. Plus, they told me I could end up going to court or jail for not going to school. I don't really believe them, 'cause my friend Bev didn't go for a long time, and they didn't do anything to her.

SP: Nothing?

A: Well, they called her house and stuff and threatened to take her to court. But they never did do anything about it.

SP: Interesting. So what are you planning to do now? You planning on coming to school more or not?

A: Oh, I'm going to come to school.

SP: Why?

A: What do you mean?

SP: Well, it sounds like it's fun to stay out of school sometimes. Plus, you said you don't think the courts will do much to you. So, I'm wondering why you're planning to come to school.

A: Well, it's not *that* much fun. Sometimes it is. It gets kind of boring at home and stuff.

SP: More boring than school?

A: Sometimes. Sometimes not.

SP: That's interesting. So you're definitely planning to come to school more now, even though it's boring sometimes?

A: Yeah.

SP: That's a big change. How are you going to make that happen?

A: I'm just gonna do what I'm doing now.

SP: You mean, set the alarm and stuff?

A: Yeah. Set the alarm and just get up in the morning. That's the big problem, getting up in the morning. See, I'm used to staying up pretty late.

SP: Yeah, I remember you saying you stayed up sometimes till 3 or 4 in the morning.

A: Yeah.

SP: Have you done that these last couple nights before coming to school?

A: Well, one night I was up till about 2. But the other night I just crashed about 11 o'clock or midnight.

SP: What would your mom say needs to happen for you to get up and get to school on time?

A: Oh, she'd probably say to keep setting the alarm in the morning. That saves her some trouble, too, 'cause she won't have to wake me.

SP: What else would she say would help you get up and get to school on time?

A: She'd say I need to go to bed earlier. She gets on me about staying up late. So I know she'd say that.

SP: How are you planning on handling this sleep thing?

A: I might just try to get to bed at 10 or something, a couple nights a week.

Discussion of Angelique's plans to maintain school attendance continued in a manner designed to clarify and empower her future plans. Conversations like this provide an opportunity for clients to reflect upon and articulate their plans to maintain desired changes. Like most of the other strategies presented in this chapter, this one capitalizes on research findings indicating that public statements or discussions of specific behavioral plans and intentions increase the likelihood of their occurrence (Ajzen & Fishbein, 1980; Madden, Ellen, & Ajzen, 1992).

Helping Clients Prepare for Relapse

Although people are naturally relieved and gratified by progress, they may also fear that improvements won't last (Duncan, 1989). Unless this is directly addressed, clients may overemphasize the significance of future setbacks and respond to them in unproductive ways. Consider the parents who used to spend 2 hours every school night verbally threatening and pleading with their fifth-grade son, Joshua, about homework. Arguments became louder and more volatile as the evening progressed, and homework remained undone. It was suggested that they "do something different" by establishing a 30-minute homework time during which they went about their other responsibilities instead of coaching Joshua's homework. Homework completion improved markedly following the parents' new plan. After 2 weeks of success, Joshua came home from school and began complaining about "stupid homework" like he used to. The parents "responded in kind" and retreated to their former ineffective tactics of verbal persuasion . . . and the problem was reborn.

School practitioners can help prevent this by suggesting that occasional relapses or slips are an inevitable part of the change process, as illustrated in the following consultation with a third-grade teacher, Mr. Carroll. Mr. Carroll and the school practitioner collaborated in developing a behavior management plan for Steven, who talked out of turn and left his seat a lot during class. The plan included brief "free times" during which Steven could engage in an activity of his choice, contingent upon short periods of acceptable classroom behavior. Steven also signed a behavior contract to this effect. The following conversation occurred 1 week after this plan was implemented, when Mr. Carroll reported small but important changes in Steven's behavior.

SCHOOL PRACTITIONER (SP): The changes you made seem to be helping.

MR. CARROLL (MR. C): Yeah. Like I said, it's not a total turn-around, but things are definitely better, not just with Steven, but with the whole class. I don't have to spend all my time redirecting him, so I have more time for teaching the rest of the students.

SP: That's great. Glad to hear it.

MR. C: Me too. (*Laughs.*)

SP: Sometimes with a change like this, things seem to go one step forward and two steps back, two more forward, and so forth. People seem to have relapses, where they slip back and start doing what they used to do. Steven might have some days like the old days when he talks out and leaves his seat a lot. I mention this so we can talk about it and maybe make a plan to deal with it if it occurs. What kinds of things can be done if Steven has bad days or bad times during class?

MR. C: Well, one thing is not to throw the behavior plan out the window right away. Maybe just try to weather it out, unless the problems continue for a whole week or something like that. Then I probably need to come up with something else.

Explicitly discussing the possibility of relapse provides an opportunity for students, parents, and teachers to prepare for setbacks by considering various ways to respond to them. We have found students, teachers, and parents to be very resourceful and creative in responding to setbacks when given the opportunity to discuss them beforehand. When clients are prepared to expect relapses, these occasions are handled more calmly and effectively and the maintenance of progress is enhanced.

Leaving the Door Open

Viewing students, teachers, and parents as competent and resourceful is integral to this approach. In doing so, we convey our confidence in their ability to maintain changes in the future. However, we do not want to close the door on the possibility of follow-up contacts that may help them sustain improvements.

When goals are reached and counseling or consultation ends, practitioners can offer follow-up booster meetings or phone calls at the client's request. Responding to criticism that brief intervention merely relieves problems without adequately addressing their underlying roots and preventing future problems, Watzlawick (1987) asserts that it is unrealistic to expect any intervention method to promise prevention of future problems. He states, "The aim of any realistic, responsible therapy can only be an increased skill in dealing with life problems as they arise, but not a problem-free life" (p. 159). Booster meetings and phone contacts help students, teachers, and parents maintain changes by (1) reminding them of "what worked" before, and (2) exploring new ways to handle the inevitable "bumps" and challenges along the road of improvement.

The following excerpt illustrates "leaving the door open" for a teacher. This was the last of three short consultations with Ms. Walters over a 3-week period. During this time, she had implemented a school–home note program (Kelley, 1990) to improve the disruptive classroom behavior of a kindergarten student, James. The student's behavior had steadily improved for 2 weeks, and the practitioner and Ms. Walters agreed to end their weekly meetings.

Ms. WALTERS (Ms. W): Thanks for your help. I really appreciate it. I was really worried there for awhile.

SCHOOL PRACTITIONER (SP): Me too. And thank you, too. Some teachers would have thrown the towel in and given up on this case, but you didn't. That takes some stamina.

Ms. W: Thank you. I'm just glad it helped.

SP: Way to go (*gives teacher high five*). Well, where do we go from here? When do you want to meet again?

Ms. W: I guess we really don't need to meet like we have been. Maybe in a few weeks.

SP: Somewhere in mid-November?

Ms. W: Yes. That sounds good.

SP: We can touch base and discuss James' situation and take it from there. If you want to talk to me before then, just give me a call and we'll set something up, okay?

Ms. W: Okay.

Booster meetings may require relatively more practitioner time compared to the other maintenance strategies, which are routinely incorporated into the intervention process. However, a short meeting or phone contact can go a long way toward maintaining progress, as well as providing useful feedback to practitioners regarding the endurance and course of previous changes.

SUMMARY

Strategies for evaluating and maintaining progress occur throughout the intervention process. Like every other component of the approach, these two tasks are driven by the "client knows best" guideline.

We believe that practical considerations are paramount in developing, selecting, and implementing strategies for evaluating and sustaining progress. Therefore, we included only those methods that have proven practical and useful in helping students, parents, and teachers to evaluate and maintain improvements in school problems.

Next, we present two full-length case studies to illustrate the entire brief intervention process from initial referral through maintenance and follow-up.

PART 3

♦♦♦

CASES AND CONCLUSIONS

♦

The Case of Larry:
Working with What Works

◆

This chapter presents the first of two start-to-finish case studies illustrating brief intervention. This case highlights the approach's competency orientation, illustrating how school practitioners can expedite change by "working with what already works" instead of focusing exclusively on the student's deficiencies.

The case of Larry is presented in the following sections: (1) referral and background, (2) assessment, (3) intervention, (4) evaluation of progress, (5) maintenance of progress; and (6) conclusion and discussion. Excerpts from meetings are provided along with commentary to clarify the approach further.

REFERRAL AND BACKGROUND

Larry was referred to the school practitioner by his teachers due to concerns regarding tardiness to class, minimal assignment completion, and disruptive behavior. He was a ninth grader in a special education program for students with mild mental disabilities. The referral was made in early November following the first grading period. Larry was described on the referral as "resistant," "oppositional," and "apathetic."

School records revealed a history of family and school problems. Larry had been in several foster homes and two facilities for children with behavior problems. Prior to enrolling in the mild mental disabilities program, he participated in programs for students with behavioral disabilities. The social services department was monitoring his school and home performance to assess the appropriateness of home placement with his father. He and his father were on a waiting list for family counseling, and he was in jeopardy of being placed in another facility, due in part to school behavior problems.

ASSESSMENT

Assessment and intervention are linked so closely in this approach that the distinction is almost arbitrary. As noted in Chapter 3, assessment expands solution opportunities by exploring and validating client experiences, goals, and resources related to the problem. Despite their interrelated nature, assessment and intervention are addressed separately for the purpose of clarity.

First Interview with Teachers

Larry's teachers were interviewed first because they initiated the request for intervention assistance. The following excerpt is from the first interview with two of Larry's teachers, Mr. Roth (Math) and Ms. Chandler (English).

SCHOOL PRACTITIONER (SP): I appreciate the information on the referral form. It would help me catch up on things to hear from both of you about what Larry is doing, or not doing, in your class that leads to trouble. Who's first?

MR. ROTH (MR. R): Where do I start? (*some laughter*) Seriously, there's so many problems. He's late to class about three times a week. When he gets there, I have to tell him to get his book out at least once. Never has homework. His behavior is the pits. He talks out whenever he feels like it, calls across the room to other students, threatens other kids. I've sent him out for cussing. And these aren't words under his breath. Everybody can hear them, including people in the hallway. Those are the biggest problems in my class.

SP: What other things is he doing, or not doing, that are causing problems in your class?

[The practitioner wants a clear, specific description of what the problem is from Mr. Roth's perspective.]

MR. R: Well, as far as "not doing," I haven't seen him work on anything in class more than a minute or so.

SP: What kinds of things?

MR. R: Mostly it's problem sheets.

SP: What are problem sheets?

MR. R: I call them problem sheets and they do them three or four times a week. A lot of times, he doesn't even attempt to do it.

SP: Do you think he has the math skills to do the sheets?

MR. R: I think he can do it. To be honest, he's done so little, it's hard to say.

SP: I know there's a bunch of stuff going on. Like you said earlier, where do you start? Of all the problems you mentioned, which one would you like to see changed the most?

[This question seeks to validate Mr. Roth's perception of multiple problems, and to explore his opinion of what needs to change first.]

MR. R: Definitely the behavior. Something needs to happen fast. I don't see how he can stay in my class, or this program, unless he gets his act together fast.

Ms. CHANDLER (Ms. C): I agree. His behavior is my biggest concern, although it's real disruptive to the class when he comes in late because he usually talks to someone in the hall real loud, then comes in and plops in his seat, taps on his desk, says something rude to a student. Stuff like that really disrupts things when you're just starting a lesson or explaining an assignment. Then he mutters stuff like, "This sucks," or "This is stupid," under his breath when I give them an assignment.

SP: When he comes in late, what happens?

Ms. C: You mean what does he do next?

SP: Him, you, other students. Yeah. I'm just trying to get a picture of what it looks like when this happens. Like if I was a fly on the wall, what would I see first, then next, and so on, after he comes in the room late?

[In addition to obtaining a concrete description of the problem behavior, it is important to explore and clarify behavioral sequences and patterns surrounding it. This information can aid in developing interventions that interrupt the problem pattern and foster different, more productive responses.]

Ms. C: Well, usually I tell him he'll need an admit slip from the Discipline Office by the end of the day for being late. He just sighs or shrugs his shoulders. He's walked out a couple times, usually muttering something under his breath about the school or me. I try to ignore some of it, but it's so loud sometimes that I can't. Plus I don't want all the other students thinking they can get away with the same kind of stuff. He flies off the handle so easy.

SP: I see what you mean. It's like a Catch-22.

Ms. C: Exactly. I don't know what to do. And I can't teach 18 other students with all this going on.

SP: What else have you tried?

Ms. C: I've talked with him a couple times to try and figure out why he's so angry.

SP: How did that work?

Ms. C: Well, he's better one to one, but he just kind of shrugged and said he didn't know why he did this stuff. I told him he was heading for more problems unless something changed.

SP: Did his behavior change at all after you talked to him?

Ms. C: Not really. Maybe a little, but it didn't last.

SP: You mentioned anger before. Could you tell me what you mean?

[The intent of this question is twofold. First, it conveys the practitioner's respect for Ms. Chandler's theory regarding the problem. Second, it may yield important information about her position on the problem and its potential solution. This information must be considered in developing interventions that are sensible and acceptable to her.]

Ms. C: I don't know what else it could be. He just seems so angry. I just figured, maybe if he talked about it, you know, got it out, maybe he'd be better. He wouldn't think we were so against him.

SP: I see what you mean. I can check that out when I meet with him. How much work does he do in English?

Ms. C: Not much. Sometimes he'll come in and get his paper out and start working. Most of the time he comes in and sits there, says something rude to another student, or lays his head on the desk.

[The observation that Larry "sometimes" does work is a small but potentially important exception. If he gets his paper out and does some work "sometimes," then perhaps he could do it a little more the next week, and so on. This exception is explored below.]

SP: What's different about those times when he gets his paper out and does more work?

Ms. C: I wish I knew. (*Laughs.*)

SP: Yeah. If you knew, you'd be on Donahue, right?

Ms. C: Right.

SP: I mean, I wonder whether it makes a difference whether it's a certain type of assignment, or maybe he's sitting in a different spot, something like that. I don't know. Can you think of anything like that that might give us a clue about what's going on when he gets his paper out?

Ms. C: No. Not really. Not offhand.

SP: What would you think of observing things during the times when he does a little better in classroom behavior or assignments? Things like what type of assignment it is, who he's sitting next to, and anything else you think might be important.

[This task is useful in two respects. First, it does not require a lot of teacher time or a change in classroom routine. Second, it invites the teacher to focus on positive behaviors and related circumstances.

This competency focus on exceptions may lead to interventions that encourage "more of" what is already working.]

Ms. C: I can try that. Anything that will help.

SP: Mr. Roth, would it be possible to make these kind of observations in your class?

Mr. R: I guess so. I can try, but I don't want to see this thing carried out for months, and us be sitting here again scratching our heads wondering what to do, you know?

SP: Yeah. I think things have reached a point where everybody's kind of at wits' end, including Mr. Becker [the school principal]. I'm going to call Larry's father and tell him about our meeting, ask for any input and suggestions he might have. I'll also meet with Larry. I have to say, as frustrated as you all are, dealing with this day in and day out, it's real impressive that you're still willing to meet to even discuss it, much less to consider ways to change it. I'll meet with Larry and his dad, and I'll contact you by next Tuesday with an update. Anything else?

Mr. R: No.

Ms. C: No.

SP: Thanks. Appreciate it.

Larry's other teachers were contacted briefly for added input, and the information from the above interview was summarized for them. The behavioral perceptions and priorities of these other teachers closely matched those of Ms. Chandler and Mr. Roth, with the exception of his social studies teacher, Ms. Smith. Ms. Smith reported that he was not rude to her or other students in the class. When asked about her ideas regarding why his behavior was relatively more acceptable in her class than others, she said that she occasionally joked with him and he seemed to like it.

Teacher interviews collectively resulted in the following goals: (1) to increase the number of times Larry arrived to class on time, (2) to increase the number of class periods during which Larry behaved acceptably, and (3) to increase the number of academic assignments completed with adequate accuracy. Teachers were asked to record some baseline observations on a form that was collaboratively developed by Mr. Roth, Ms. Chandler, and the school practitioner. The form required rating Larry's daily performance in each of the three goal areas by circling a "yes" or "no" to indicate whether or not the behavior represented "an improvement" over the first month of school and "was acceptable" to them. These rating criteria were not highly detailed and refined. However, the form was user friendly, applicable to all of his classes, and, perhaps most importantly, designed primarily by the teachers themselves.

First Interview with Larry's Father

Larry's father was unable to meet at school. He was contacted by phone to invite his input and to share information from the teacher interviews. When asked for his advice on how to help Larry in school, he stated that he had tried talking to Larry and witholding privileges. Withholding privileges made things worse. The talks helped the two of them get along at home for a few days, but did not change things at school. Mr. Brown said he had not discovered what improved schoolwork or school behavior, but would be willing to try anything.

Mr. Brown explained that he had to work a long second shift, making it difficult for him to be of much help to Larry on school matters. He also had difficulty reading himself. Mr. Brown asked the school practitioner to meet with Larry to try and help him in school. He also said that he wanted Larry to remain living with him. The practitioner thanked him for his time and information, and agreed to meet with Larry.

First Interview with Larry

When Larry arrived to meet with the school practitioner, he hunkered down in the chair, pulled his hat over his forehead, stared at the floor, and said, "This school sucks." The following conversation proceeded from there.

SCHOOL PRACTITIONER (SP): Do you have an idea why they asked me to talk with you?

LARRY (L): (*Shrugs shoulders and shakes head, indicating "no."*)

SP: Well, some of your teachers want to see changes in things like getting to class on time and doing some more work in class. Does that surprise you any?

L: (*Shakes head, indicating "no."*)

SP: Would you prefer me to ask "yes or no" type questions so that you can just nod your head to answer if you don't feel like talking?

L: I can talk.

SP: Okay. Well, I kind of told you what the teachers were wanting. My question is, what do *you* want?

L: I want to get out of this fucking school.

SP: Have you figured out a way to do that?

L: (*Looks at the practitioner for the first time during the entire interview, appearing somewhat surprised by the question.*) No. Well, they suspend me sometimes, but it just lasts for a few days, like 2 days or something.

SP: Would you like it to last longer?

[The practitioner neither argues with Larry nor makes any assumptions about his goals or positions. In addition to establishing a collaborative relationship, this cooperative stance is often recognized by students as "something different" than the lecture-oriented, authoritative format of many previous interactions with adults regarding the problem.]

L: Well, kind of, but not really. 'Cause, if I get kicked out, I could get in a lot of trouble.

As the conversation unfolded, Larry became more talkative. He described various foster homes and treatment facilities he had been in, stating a strong desire not to return to either. He did not elaborate on details regarding his mother's absence, or his father's temporary custody. However, he stated his desire to remain with his father. He said that he wanted to "stay where he was at and not get sent away." The practitioner informed him of the conversations with his teachers and father, including the goals developed by his teachers.

Collaborative goal formulation is a crucial initial step in promoting efficient change. A clear understanding of students' goals from *their* perspective, and in *their* words, allows practitioners to validate these goals and strengthen the alliance throughout the intervention process. We have found that impasses in the change process result mainly from practitioners' failure to accept and cooperate with client goals.

The importance of cooperative relationships between school practitioners and adolescents cannot be overstated. Teenagers often perceive adults' efforts to "help them" as power plays designed to usurp their independence or coerce them into compliance (Brigham, 1989). Wexler (1991) states, "When adolescents feel forced into something, they resist. On the other hand, when they feel that they are choosing to do something for their own self-interest, their motivation can be intense" (p. 94). Wexler's point is applicable to students of any age, as well as teachers and parents.

The following excerpt illustrates the process of client-directed goal formulation.

SP: What needs to happen so you won't get sent away?

L: I don't know. I guess if I stop getting in trouble here.

SP: What else would help you stay where you're at?

L: I don't know. They [social services caseworkers] tell me I'll get sent away if I keep getting in trouble at school.

SP: So, what can you do at school to help you stay where you're at?

L: Well, I guess that stuff they said about being late to class and talking and stuff.

SP: You mean the stuff your teachers said was causing problems?

L: Yeah.

[The discussion led to the formulation of specific behavioral goals consistent with those developed by the teachers.]

The five-E method of utilizing exceptions, described in Chapter 4, played a key role in this case. This method includes (1) *eliciting* exceptions to the problem, (2) *elaborating* upon the details and circumstances of the exception, (3) *expanding* the exception to occur more frequently or in other contexts, (4) *evaluating* the effectiveness of exception-based interventions, and (5) *empowering* and maintaining desired changes.

The following exchange illustrates *eliciting* exceptions to the problem.

SP: So, you actually want to stay in school?

L: Yeah. I don't want to get sent away.

SP: That makes sense. Do you want to see if we can come up things that might help you not get sent away so you can stay with your father and stay in school?

L: Yeah. Like what?

SP: I don't know. Tell me about the times at school when you don't get in trouble as much.

L: I never get in trouble, well, (*laughs*) not a lot, in Ms. Smith's class.

SP: Really?

L: Yeah.

SP: What subject do you have Ms. Smith for?

L: Social studies.

[Once an exception is identified, the task shifts to *elaborating* upon it to clarify the conditions under which it occurred. The details and circumstances related to the exception can form the basis of interventions that encourage Larry, and his teachers, to do "more of" what is already working.]

SP: What's so different about Ms. Smith's class than your other classes?

L: I don't know, she's nicer. We get along good.

SP: What exactly does she do that's nicer?

L: I don't know, she's just nice. She says "Hi" to me when I come to class. She doesn't hassle me like the other teachers. We got some real jerk teachers in this school.

SP: What else does she do that's nice?

L: She checks up on me to see how I'm doing on stuff. Like, she'll walk by my desk and ask if I need help on anything.

SP: What else?

L: I guess that's it.

SP: How about her class, or the stuff you study in social studies? Do you like social studies?

L: Not really. It's pretty boring.

SP: What else is different about Ms. Smith, or her class, or the kind of work you do in her class?

L: The work's easier in her class, and she helps you with it. She doesn't give you as much stuff to do. It's, like, one sheet.

[Previous teacher interviews indicated that he had not successfully completed an assignment in any class for the past month except Ms. Smith's, where he completed half the assignments. The details and circumstances of the "Ms. Smith exception" are summarized as follows: (1) she greeted him when he came into the class; (2) she gave him "easier work" that he was capable of doing; and (3) she approached his desk periodically to see how he was doing on an assignment. These elements were carefully noted by the practitioner for their potential application by other teachers.]

Larry also was asked what *he* did differently in Ms. Smith's class as a way of further elaborating on the exception.

SP: So, how are *you* different in Ms. Smith's class. How is it that you manage to pretty much stay out of trouble in that class?

L: I just do my work. I like the class, so I do my work.

SP: More than you do in other classes?

L: A lot more.

SP: Do you get to class on time more in Ms. Smith's than in your other classes?

L: Yeah. She's real nice. She stands by the door and says "Hi" to everybody that comes in. See, that's what I mean, she's nicer.

SP: Okay. She's nicer, but *you* also do things different in her class, right? You're different, I mean you act different, in her class, right?

L: Right.

SP: How are you different there?

L: I don't know, I guess I just get there on time.

SP: What do you mean?

L: You know, I get there before the late bell rings. So, I don't get sent out for being late.

SP: Wow, that must be hard for you to do, 'cause you've been late for class pretty much this year, right?

L: Yeah.

SP: How do you get yourself there on time?

L: I just go to my locker right from lunch, and go straight to the class.

SP: Do you go straight to the other classes?

L: (*Laughs.*) No. I'll see some people in the hall and talk and stuff.

SP: This is really wild. This is really something. So, it's not like it's something you *can't* do, like you can't get there in time to classes, but it's more like a choice or something you decide on. Is that true?

L: Yeah. If I want to go, I go. I just usually don't feel like going to class.

SP: Well, I imagine it's still hard to do even if you want to, isn't it?

L: A little. I mean, I just don't like the other classes, so I'm late and I screw off more.

SP: Do you think being on time, paying attention better, stuff like that, more like you're doing in social studies, is helping your chances of staying where you're at with your dad and not getting sent to another one of those places?

[The practitioner makes no assumptions and takes nothing for granted, preferring to "hear it from Larry." These questions invite Larry to state specifically what he is already doing towards his goal of staying with his father and not getting sent away. Questions about what *he* is doing to make it better in Ms. Smith's class further clarify the circumstances of the exception.]

L: I think, well, I know, if I do more stuff like come to class, be on time, like that, it will help.

SP: So, it's like whatever you do in Ms. Smith's class is helping you not get sent away, helping you stay in school, do decent work, you know, so that you won't get sent away. Is that true?

L: Yeah.

INTERVENTION

The initial meetings with Larry, his teachers, and his father provided ample direction and material for developing interventions aimed at utilizing exceptions to the problem.

Intervention with Larry

Larry's comments in the initial interview paved the way for exploring how he might *expand* his "exception behavior" in Ms. Smith's class to other classes.

SP: I wonder how you could do some of that same stuff in your other classes?

[The practitioner "wonders" instead of "instructing" or "directing" Larry about the possibility of expanding successful behavior to other classes. A tentative presentation of ideas and interventions conveys Larry's freedom to accept or reject them without challenge. If a suggestion is rejected, the practitioner simply "moves on" and offers another instead of trying to convince Larry of its merits or of his impending doom should he not follow it.]

L: I guess I could just do it.

SP: It seems to me like it would be really hard to all of a sudden change that quick. What do you think?

L: I don't know. Yeah, maybe.

SP: Would you be willing to try doing "Ms. Smith behavior" in one of your other classes?

[The practitioner invites Larry to consider a small change, based on the systemic notion that small changes lead to larger ones in domino fashion.]

L: I get it. I see what you mean. So I could come to English class on time and behave, without screwing around and stuff.

SP: Yeah. What do you think about that?

L: I think I can do it. I could do it in my other classes, too.

SP: Well, it's up to you, but that's a big change. You don't want to bite off more than you can chew, you know.

[In addition to acknowledging the challenge of making big changes in school behavior, this comment (1) allows Larry to "save face" with the practitioner if he is unsuccessful, and (2) strengthens the practitioner's collaborative, noncoercive position. This comment also differed from the "change or else" position of Larry's father and teachers. If the "change or else" position worked, the referral would not have been made in the first place.]

Larry said he would try "being on time," "doing more work," and "not screwing around" in English and history class. He and the practitioner further discussed some specific behaviors that comprised these terms.

Intervention with Teachers

The practitioner told the teachers about the meeting with Larry, asking each of them about the possibility of implementing some of the strategies that were associated with Larry arriving to class on time, paying attention better, and getting more work done. These strategies included (1) greeting him in a friendly way, (2) reducing the quantity of work or breaking it into smaller units; and (3) periodically approaching him to monitor his work and ask if he needed help. Some teachers elected not to change their existing instruction or interactions with Larry substantially. However, every teacher agreed to implement at least one of the above strategies.

EVALUATION OF PROGRESS

Larry's teachers rated his performance for 3 months, from late October through January. All but two of the teachers documented ratings on a daily basis. Substantial changes in teacher perceptions of
Larry's school performance were indicated. Whereas typical baseline ratings indicated "acceptable" behavior in only one or two of
the six class periods, he received "acceptable" ratings on the average
of four to five periods per day for 3 months following intervention.
Formal disciplinary infractions decreased by 80% following intervention.

In addition to evaluating progress by examining teacher ratings, the "social validity" (Wolf, 1978) of these changes was assessed
by asking Larry and his teachers how "important" the changes were
in everyday school life. As noted in Chapter 6, it is important to go
beyond ratings and other evaluation data to determine if clients actually experience the *practical significance* of changes in the problem.
The notion of social validity is consistent with the client-directed
nature of brief intervention. Both Larry and his teachers viewed the
changes as significant in contributing to his overall school performance.

MAINTENANCE OF PROGRESS

Brief contacts with Larry and his teachers following these changes
were aimed at *empowering and maintaining* progress.

Empowering and Maintaining Progress with Larry

The following is an excerpt from a conversation in December intended to help Larry clarify and maintain desired changes.

SP: Wow. Look at these ratings. What's going on here?

L: Doing my work. Trying instead of just sitting there. I'm not
messing with other kids as much.

SP: This is pretty different than the way it used to be, isn't it?

L: Yeah. A lot different. You can ask the principal of my school last year how much trouble I've been in there. Man, all the time.

SP: You were in trouble a lot down there?

L: All the time. I'd get suspended for 3 days. Get suspended, come back, get suspended again.

SP: When's the last time you been suspended up here?

L: Uh, September. Yeah, September, I think.

[Records indicated that Larry had been suspended on four separate occasions—two in September and two in October. He had not been suspended since that time.]

SP: I'm just amazed. When I see somebody that's made a change like you have, I always wonder how it was done. I want to know how you did those things.

L: Man, I can't believe how I straightened up this year.

SP: Yeah. How did you change like this?

L: I don't know, I just wanted to. I want to do better. Not sit there at the Discipline Office all day.

[The practitioner continued "blaming" Larry for the positive changes, asking specifically what he had done to bring them about. Larry's tone of voice was energetic and animated during this discussion, quite a change from his original presentation of slumping in the chair, staring at the floor, and nodding "yes" or "no" to the practitioner's questions.]

The practitioner continued blaming Larry for success as the focus of conversation shifted to how things were different between Larry and his teachers. In the next excerpt, Larry reports a change in his view of teachers. The practitioner follows this lead by exploring the connection between Larry's behavior and the way he is treated by teachers and other students.

L: My teachers are getting cooler, too.

SP: What do you mean?

L: Well, they're just cooler. Like, they're cooler with me. Nicer and stuff.

SP: Why do you think they treat you nicer?

L: I guess I'm treating them nicer. (*Laughs.*)

SP: That makes sense. How do you treat them nicer?

L: Just by not smartin' off, and trying to do better and stuff.

SP: So, you think you can actually kind of control what your teachers do by the way you act?

L: What?

SP: Well, like when you do better, your teachers are cooler, right?

L: Yeah.

SP: So, you kind of control their coolness by the way you act in class. When you're cool in class, it makes them cooler.

L: Yeah.

SP: Yeah. You never thought you could control teachers, did you?

L: (*laughs*) No.

SP: How about other students? Are things any different with them?

L: Not really. Well, maybe a little. They don't tease me and mess with me like they used to. You see, this one kid, Marcus, he teases, tries to cap on me a lot. He's cooler now.

The discussion continued to explore other changes in his relationships with students and school staff. He commented that even the school principal, whom he had previously viewed as "out to get him" and "on his case all the time," was nicer to him recently. Next, the practitioner attempts to help Larry clarify his plans to maintain progress and to prepare for possible relapses in the future.

SP: Do you plan to keep doing these things?

L: Yeah.

SP: What can you do to make that happen?

L: What?

SP: What can you do to keep things going good?

L: Uh, come to class and keep getting good ratings and stuff. Not smart off, do my work.

SP: So you plan to keep doing the things you're doing now in class to keep getting good ratings and be able to stay in school and not get sent away?

[The practitioner explicitly refers to Larry's goal, stated in his own words, throughout the process to emphasize that it is *his* goal that dictates the nature and content of intervention, evaluation, and maintenance.]

L: Yeah.

SP: You know, changes like this, big changes that are really hard to do, like the kind you've made in school, sometimes go a little back and forth. I mean, like you have real good days or even whole weeks that are pretty good. Then, you have a bad day when it's just like it used to be.

L: Yeah, like last Friday right before we got out. I kind of lost it in math. Marcus said something about my dad, and I told him to get fucked. I didn't scream it, I mean, like I used to, but Mr. Roth heard it and kind of got on me, made me apologize and stuff. I told him what happened and he made Marcus apologize to me. I said, "That's cool, he got in trouble, too." Which he should've, 'cause he started it.

SP: Yeah, so, things like that will probably happen now and then. How did you do during the rest of that class?

L: What?

SP: I mean, after that happened with Marcus, were you cool, did you do okay in class after that happened?

L: I just sat there and didn't look at Marcus no more.

SP: And you made it through the class without any more trouble?

L: Yeah.

SP: That's great. I mean, that you made it through without losing it again. Three months ago you might of really lost it and got suspended or something.

L: Yeah. I might of smacked him.

SP: So, when things sometimes go bad during a class, or somebody says something to you or about your dad or your family, you can stay cool and hold it together so you don't get sent to the office.

L: Yeah.

The conversation continued exploring ways that Larry could effectively prepare for and handle relapses in school behavior. He came up with several ideas, including (1) looking away from people that tease him, such as by looking out the window or at his paper during class; (2) taking a deep breath when he feels himself getting mad; and (3) saying "sorry" when he "messes up" in class instead of storming out or "cussing out" the teacher or other students. Additional details of these strategies were discussed, including specific ways to apologize to students and teachers, and practical deep breathing strategies that he could do in a few seconds right in the classroom. The practitioner "kept the door open" by offering follow-up meetings at Larry's request to help him maintain progress.

Empowering and Maintaining Progress with Teachers

Positive blame can be assigned to teachers as well as students following desired changes. The following conversation occurred with Larry's English teacher (Ms. C) following improvements.

Ms. C: Things aren't perfect by any means, but a lot better.

SP: What do you attribute the changes to?

Ms. C: Well, maybe me making the first move and making a point of saying something positive to him early in the class period made a difference. He still has a lot of trouble with the work, but we don't argue as much and it's more like we're on the same side instead of enemies.

SP: I imagine it was pretty hard to make these changes, after all the hassles you had with him.

Ms. C: Not really. I was willing to do anything that would help calm the situation down so it wasn't like a tug of war to get him to cooperate. I'm just glad it's working.

SP: Yeah. These changes you made in your approach to him—are you planning to continue with these?

Ms. C: Definitely. It's the schoolwork now that I need to look at.

Ms. Chandler and the practitioner proceeded to explore ways to address Larry's difficulty with certain assignments, along with ways to maintain the instructional and interactional changes that seemed to be working well. Similar discussions occurred with some of Larry's other teachers following his improvements.

Empowering and Maintaining Progress with Mr. Brown

When informed by the school practitioner of the positive changes in Larry's school behavior, Mr. Brown expressed great appreciation for the work of school personnel. He said that Larry seemed more interested in school, and that the two of them actually had some "decent discussions" about school for the first time in months. When asked what he had been doing in recent weeks, he said he was not "getting on" Larry as much about school, because it usually led to arguments and didn't change things at school. The practitioner encouraged him to continue with this approach because, based on his report, it worked, and complimented Mr. Brown for coming up with this effective plan. The practitioner offered his availability for future assistance with Larry's school performance at Mr. Brown's request.

CONCLUSION AND DISCUSSION

Although there were occasional disciplinary infractions throughout the remainder of the school year, their frequency and nature were much less problematic as compared to the beginning of the year. Larry was never suspended following intervention. His major goals of remaining at school and at home with his father were attained, and he successfully passed to 10th grade.

This case demonstrates the advantage of "working with what works" in the process of developing interventions for school problems. Building upon thoughts, actions, and resources that are *already* contributing to client goals, if only just a little, is often an efficient pathway to change.

Instead of following suit with previous solution attempts to lecture, threaten, and otherwise "stamp out the problem," the practitioner focused on small but important exceptions. This case also illustrates that interventions developed directly from the ideas, competencies, and resources of clients typically are more effective and acceptable to them than interventions that are largely dictated by the practitioner and imposed on clients. Assuming an accommodating, collaborative position activates the "client factors" and "relationship factors" that contribute so significantly to success (Garfield, 1994; Lambert, 1992).

Even in chronic problem situations such as Larry's case, it is possible to "work with what works" by focusing on exceptions and competencies in the pursuit of client goals. This case, like every other one presented in this book, illustrates that people can make amazing changes when provided with the opportunity and encouragement to discover their own solutions.

CHAPTER 8

The Case of Maria:
When Rationality
Doesn't Make Sense

♦

Most significant school-related problems are highly noticeable and bothersome to school personnel. In the case of Maria, school personnel were totally unaware of the problem, despite the fact that it turned her household upside down.

Maria's case highlights both major intervention guidelines. The "client knows best" guideline is evidenced by the exploration and validation of parent and student beliefs about the problem and its potential solution. The second intervention guideline, "if at first you don't succeed, try something different," stresses the importance of interrupting repetitive problem patterns in order to allow for more productive responses. This guideline is prominent in Maria's case.

REFERRAL AND BACKGROUND

Ms. Jordan contacted the practitioner in late January regarding Maria, her 10-year-old daughter. Maria was a fourth-grader in a program for academically gifted students. Her school history was characterized by consistently strong grades (A's) in all academic subjects. Report cards noted that she was a polite, quiet, hardworking student who cooperated well with teacher requests and school requirements. Maria lived at home with her parents and younger brother, James.

Approximately 2 weeks before Ms. Jordan's first phone call to the practitioner, Maria began complaining of headaches and stomachaches. She frequently asked her parents to take her temperature in the morning on school days, and her complaints became progressively stronger and more frequent. She began insisting on staying up later at night, arguing with her parents when they directed her to go to bed. Mornings and bedtimes had never been a problem in the past. Upon arriving at school, Maria often pleaded with her father not to make her go in. Sometimes she would cling to the car door, requiring her father to coax her verbally and physically from the car into school.

Maria was examined by a pediatrician to assess her complaints regarding headaches and stomachaches. No physical difficulties were noted. Her grades for the first semester, and on a recent "progress report card," were consistently high. The parents had not received any calls from the school regarding Maria's academic performance or behavior.

The case occurred over a period of 3 weeks, consisting of two individual meetings with Maria, one initial interview with Ms. Jordan, and four phone contacts with Ms. Jordan.

ASSESSMENT

Much of the background information above was gathered during the first interview with Ms. Jordan. The next section covers additional aspects of that interview.

First Interview with Ms. Jordan

Excerpts from the school practitioner's first interview with Ms. Jordan, and related commentary, are presented below.

Ms. JORDAN (Ms. J): Like I told you on the phone, she's had almost completely straight A's since kindergarten, and all of the sudden she has this school phobia thing. We don't know what's happening, or what to do with her. It's scary. That's why I thought it would help if someone else talked with her. It's just really weird. We don't know what to do.

SCHOOL PRACTITIONER (SP): Yeah, sounds pretty weird. Scary, too.

Like you've watched her pretty much cruise through school with no big problems, and now this.

Ms. J: Yeah.

[The practitioner acknowledges and mirrors Ms. J's perception of the unusual ("weird") and alarming ("scary") nature of Maria's recent behavior.]

SP: You said "we" don't know what to do. Who else besides you?

Ms. J: My husband Paul and I. He's been trying to talk to her about this stuff. I've taken counseling courses too, and here we are. Makes you feel pretty dumb. We don't know what to do. So I finally said, "We've got to get some help on this." That's when I called you.

SP: I'm glad you called. I don't how it is with your kids, but with mine, this psychology and counseling stuff doesn't always help.

Ms. J: (*Laughs.*) Yeah, I know.

SP: It's a lot easier for me to calmly listen to someone else's problem and think of ideas for them, but it's a lot harder with my own problems or my kids' problems.

[The practitioner's "one-downing" self-disclosure is intended to validate Ms. Jordan's experience and frustration, and to establish his role as "collaborator" versus "expert" on the problem.]

Ms. J: Exactly. That's why we're so frustrated. She's obviously troubled a lot by something, and it's, like, we should be able to help her, but we can't. We've tried everything. The weird thing is, nobody at school has even called, and she says she's doing fine in school.

SP: Yeah. That's interesting. I want to find out about some of those things you've tried, but first it would help me to get a better handle on the things she's doing, or not doing, that concern you the most right now.

[Before moving on, the practitioner wants to get a clear idea of the specific behaviors, or lack of behaviors, that constitute "the problem" from Ms. Jordan's perspective.]

Ms. J: Okay. Every night, she tells us she doesn't want to go to bed, and begs us to stay up later. She'll say, "Please let me stay up. I promise I'll get up in the morning." At first we didn't let her, and that didn't help. We would just have these big arguments about going to bed, and she ended up going to sleep real late anyway. So we thought, "Hey, we got nothing to lose, let's try letting her stay up an extra hour and see what happens." That didn't make any difference, either. She still argued with us about going to bed no matter when her bedtime was.

SP: So, is the biggest problem that she's staying up too late at night, or is it that she's giving you fits and arguing about it?

Ms. J: Well, this might sound selfish, but the arguing and hassles are the biggest problem, because she eventually gets to bed and gets to sleep okay. But the arguing and carrying on upsets everything. Even James [Maria's 7-year-old brother] asks her to knock it off so he can sleep.

SP: Okay. I just want to make sure we're dealing with what's most important to you. So, please excuse me for asking a bunch of questions. I just want to get a handle on exactly what's going on.

Ms. J: That's fine.

[The practitioner asks Ms. Jordan more questions about the specific nature of the problem, such as the actual comments that comprise most arguments, how long the arguments last, and so forth. Next, the patterns surrounding the problem are explored.]

SP: Do you and your husband both deal with the bedtime thing, or one of you more than the other?

Ms. J: Well, she and I have been locking horns a lot. We're more alike so I think we clash more. So my husband has been talking to her more lately. He usually tells her to go to bed about 9: 00, and she starts asking to stay up later. We say "No," she argues and cries about it sometimes, and eventually goes to bed.

SP: How does he tell her to go to bed? I mean, what does he usually say?

The conversation proceeded to clarify the interactional patterns surrounding the bedtime problem. The practitioner and Ms. Jordan also explored her concerns regarding mornings. Ms. Jordan reported that Maria "always" asked to have her temperature taken in the morning, and pleaded with her parents to stay home from school. She continued pleading with her father on the way to school in the car. During the 2 weeks preceding this interview, Mr. Jordan often verbally and physically coaxed her from the car upon arriving at school.

This discussion resulted in the following three-part "problem definition" regarding Maria's behavior: (1) asking to have her temperature taken in the morning, which she had done on every school day for the past 2 weeks; (b) pleading with her parents to let her stay up later at night; and (c) pleading with her father to take her home upon being dropped off at school in the morning, sometimes refusing to leave the car. Ms. Jordan reported that these behaviors had occurred every morning and evening on school days during the past 2 weeks or so. In the next excerpt from the same interview, the practitioner explores the parents' theories and positions on the problem, including their previous attempts to resolve it.

SP: What kind of theories do you have about what's going on with Maria?

Ms. J: Well, the only thing we can think of is that she's afraid of failing, like a fear of failure thing. Because when we've asked her what's going on, she usually says, "Oh, nothing," or "I don't know," and asks us not to bug her about it. She doesn't even want to talk about it. We tell her the reason we ask is because we care, that we're trying to help her. I don't think she really believes that.

SP: Why do you think she doesn't believe that?

Ms. J: Well, she usually gives you that blank stare, that look that means "when will this be over?" (*Laughs.*)

SP: So, what kinds of things do you and your husband usually say to her during these talks?

Ms. J: Well, I tell her how I used to be scared to go to school sometimes. I was afraid of kids picking on me, and I told her that. I'm hoping that it will help her realize that other people have been afraid, too. So, maybe my anxiety is transferring to her, like she can sense my tension about it, and that makes it worse. So, that's why my husband has been taking over lately.

SP: How does your husband approach it?

Ms. J: He's been talking to her about thinking straight, the rational thinking stuff, because she says one of her teachers is real mean and she seems real focused on this teacher. She says the teacher is real mean and yells at kids. The thing is, we asked her if the teacher has ever yelled at her, and she said, "No." She gets A's in this class, she's always been good at school. I mean she's never had one discipline problem throughout school. So, there's really no reason for her to be this afraid. She's getting A's and not getting in trouble.

SP: Does your husband talk to her about that?

Ms. J: Yeah. He's a professional counselor, and he uses rational counseling a lot in his work. And so he points out that the teacher has never really yelled at her. Plus, even if she does, how can that really hurt her? It's not something to be afraid of. As long as she studies and gets decent grades, the teacher can't really take anything away from her. We know about the teacher. She's real strict with the kids, but she's not abusive or anything like that. That's just the way she teaches. So we're trying to get Maria to be more reasonable about the whole thing. Paul tells her to think about the worst case scenario, like if she gets a B or C in this class. Big deal. We tell her, "We just want you to learn, and one B is not going to ruin your academic career." She catastrophizes the whole thing and gets herself all worked up. We want her to be able to face up to her problems and handle them, instead of trying to run away from them.

SP: So, these talks don't seem to be getting through?

Ms. J: No. I don't think so. She turns us off before we hardly start. She says, "You don't understand." Then we say, "We know we don't understand. That's what we're trying to do. But you're not telling us anything." That's how it usually goes, and we both walk away disgusted.

The discussion proceeded to explore Ms. Jordan's perspective regarding the strategy of talking to Maria. Ms. Jordan stated that these talks actually seemed to make the bedtime and morning problems worse, as well as upsetting the whole house. She requested that the school practitioner meet with her daughter, and added that Maria did not want to meet at school because "she doesn't want other kids to think she's crazy." The practitioner agreed to meet Maria at her house, and suggested that her mother present the meeting as a "discussion" or "chat" instead of a "counseling session."

Although it is not always feasible to meet people in their homes, it was in this case. The practitioner accommodated this request due to Maria's strong preference to meet at home. The following exchange occurred at the end of the initial meeting with Ms. Jordan.

SP: Before we stop, are there any other things you've tried, or even thought about trying, to turn this thing around?

[By the time parents seek counseling, they typically have given the problem, and potential solutions, a great deal of thought and effort. This question capitalizes on their resources and ideas, even those that have not yet been applied to the problem. The practitioner–client alliance also is strengthened by ongoing requests for client ideas.]

Ms. J: No. The stuff I told you, that's about it.

SP: Well, please think about that, and if you think of anything, give me a call, because we might be able to build on something you've already tried that works, or something you've thought of trying but haven't got around to yet. Okay?

Ms. J: Okay. I'll let you know if I come up with anything. We'll do whatever it takes.

First Interview with Maria

When the practitioner arrived at Maria's house, she was sitting at the dining room table playing a computer game. Ms. Jordan introduced them and left the room. Maria continued silently playing the game with her back to the practitioner for about 15 minutes. The practitioner said nothing during this time. Maria suddenly turned around, looked at the practitioner, and said, "Okay, I'm ready." The following conversation begins at that point.

SCHOOL PRACTITIONER (SP): Okay. I'm glad you decided to go ahead with this chat. I talked to your mother a few days ago. She said things were pretty uptight around here lately.

MARIA (M): (*Nods head, indicating "yes."*)

SP: Do you want things to change?

M: (*Nods head, indicating "yes."*)

SP: How much of a problem do you see this as being? Say, on a scale from 1 to 100, 1 being "no problem whatsoever," and 100 being "a big, big problem," where would you put it?

M: 75.

SP: 75. Okay. What do you think your mom would say?

M: I don't know. You can ask her.

SP: Good point. Who do you think is more concerned about things– you, your mom, your dad, or James [younger brother]?

M: James? He doesn't care. I'd say my mom or dad first, then me.

SP: Do you think your mom and dad have reason to be as concerned as they are?

M: No. Well, some reason. But they make such a big deal of it.

SP: What could they do to be of more help to you right now?

M: Just drop the school thing for awhile. My dad keeps saying, "You're not being reasonable, you're not being reasonable." I get tired of hearing it. It bugs me. It makes it worse.

SP: Makes what worse?

M: The school thing.

SP: What exactly is the school thing?

M: You said you talked to my mother. Didn't she tell you?

SP: She told me that you ask to have your temperature taken a lot, and you ask them to stay up at night and to not make you go to school.

M: That's it.

SP: Anything you want to add to that?

M: No, that's pretty well it.

SP: Your mom said things aren't going real well with one of your teachers.

M: That's one way of putting it.

SP: How would you put it?

M: She's a witch, basically. She never smiles, she never talks to anybody except to yell at them. A real joy.

SP: Sounds like it. How long has this yelling and stuff been going on?

M: All year.

SP: Wow. How have you been able to stand it up to now?

M: It's not easy.

The practitioner's question implies *acceptance* of Maria's characterization of the teacher. "Acceptance" is not the same as "agreement." The purpose of this relationship is to facilitate change, not to promote consensus between the opinions of Maria and the practitioner, or to convert Maria to the practitioner's theory of the problem. The distinction between acceptance and agreement is crucial in brief intervention. The practitioner accepts and works within clients' theories and opinions because this is more effective in promoting change than trying to "sell them" on a different theory or perspective (Conoley, Ivey, Conoley, Scheel, & Bishop, 1992). Coercive attempts to force people into different positions typically lead to "resistance" and impede change (Haley, 1987).

The practitioner continues to explore and validate Maria's perceptions of the teacher.

SP: On that scale again, how mean would you say this teacher is, where 1 is, like, the nicest teacher there is, and 100 is the meanest?

M: You mean I can't go over 100? (*Laughs.*)

SP: (*Laughs.*) No, you can't go over 100.

M: 95. No, 97.

SP: Wow. Mean city, huh?

M: Totally.

SP: How do you manage to deal with this? Your mom told me your grades have been keeping up in that class and in your other subjects. How do you do that?

M: I try not to think about it.

SP: About what?

M: About her.

SP: Does that help?

M: No.

SP: What do you mean?

SP: It doesn't help. I try not to think about her, but I keep thinking about her.

SP: Is it like the more you try not to think about her, the more you think about her?

M: Yep.

SP: How do you know it's not working when you try to not think about her?

M: I just keep thinking about her when I try not to. I get all nervous in class. I even sweat.

[Maria's attempted solution of "trying not to think" about the mean teacher had become part of the problem as she continued to apply it despite its ineffectiveness.]

SP: So, what else have you tried?

M: That's it.

SP: What do you want to see happen with this school thing?

M: I just want it to be like it was. I mean, I never liked her in the first place, but this is crazy. I just want to go in her class and do the stuff without thinking about her.

At this point, the practitioner and Maria began discussing an "experiment" that she could try in the mean teacher's class. This experiment was an integral aspect of intervention, and is described later.

Assessment Summary: The Building Blocks of Intervention

The interactions and information described above provided a rich foundation for intervention. Key discoveries that emerged from initial interviews are summarized below as they relate to clients' (1) previous solution attempts, (2) goals, and (3) positions or "theories" regarding the problem and its potential solution.

Previous Solution Attempts

The major theme of parental solution attempts was to instruct Maria regarding the irrationality of her fears about the teacher. As the problem became worse, the parents responded with "more of the same." They refined and strengthened their "solution" by incorporating additional terminology and strategies of rational counseling. Maria's attempted solution was "trying not to think" about the teacher. The harder she tried not to think about the teacher, the more nervous she became and "a problem was born."

It appeared that the attempts of Maria and her parents to resolve the problem actually made it worse. They were stuck in what the MRI term a "vicious problem cycle" (Watzlawick et al., 1974). Successful intervention would need to interrupt these ineffective solution attempts in order to promote different, more productive responses to the problem.

Goals

When asked specifically how she would know when things were improving, Ms. Jordan said that she and her husband would see a decrease in the frequency and intensity of Maria's three problem behaviors: (1) asking to have her temperature taken, (2) pleading with her parents to stay up past her bedtime, and (3) pleading with her father to take her home instead of dropping her off at school in the morning. In addition to providing a clear indicator of goal attainment, parents' observations of these behaviors were incorporated into interventions described later.

Maria's wanted to "not worry so much" at school and "get things back to the way they were." Maria declined the invitation to specify these goals further. For example, in response to the question, "How will you know things are starting to get better and back to where they used to be?" Maria stated, "I'll just know. That's a weird question." The practitioner accepted this rather than pushing it, and suggested that she rate how things were going on a scale of 1 to 100, where 1 is "the pits," and 100 is "the greatest." Maria agreed to do this.

Positions or "Theories"

School personnel expressed no concerns whatsoever regarding Maria or her school performance. The parents' position was revealed in the initial interview with Ms. Jordan. They viewed Maria as troubled and in need of "support." Ms. Jordan said that they wanted Maria to learn to "face up to" and "handle" her problems instead of running away from them. Both parents were actively involved in helping Maria and remained willing to do "whatever it takes."

Maria thought that her parents were overreacting by "making a big deal" of the "school thing." Although she did not express the same level of urgency as her parents, Maria definitely wanted things to change "back to the way they used to be." She viewed her math teacher, Ms. Minton, as extremely domineering and "mean."

The information regarding previous solution attempts, goals, and positions provided a clear direction for intervention.

INTERVENTION

The seamless link between assessment and intervention is illustrated by the practitioner's incorporation of goals and positions held by Maria and her parents into interventions designed to interrupt their ineffective solution attempts.

Intervention with Maria

The following exchange illustrates the practitioner's aim to interrupt Maria's ineffective solution attempts in a way that honored her goal and position. This is a continuation of the first meeting at Maria's house.

SP: I'm wondering if you could help me get a better handle on just how mean Ms. Minton is by keeping track of how many mean things she does during class.

[The practitioner presents this suggestion from the "one-down" perspective of "needing Maria's help" to understand her situation fully. This validates her view of the teacher, and provides the opportunity for her to assume the role of "helper" instead of "helpee."]

M: (*Smiles.*) What?

SP: It would be like an experiment to measure meanness. Like in science, where they do experiments and observe and keep track of things. You would have to observe real close so you don't miss anything. I could get a better idea of how mean she is if you would make a small mark in your notebook every time she does something mean. Remember, this is just observing and marking, not doing anything about it. Just observing and making the mean marks so we know what we're dealing with.

[This intervention task acknowledged and fit Maria's preoccupation with the teacher's critical style. If implemented, it would interrupt previous solution attempts by "requiring" her to pay close attention to the teacher's "meanness," thereby blocking her unproductive efforts to "try not to think" about it. The emphasis on "just observing and marking" and not "doing anything about it" differed from the urgency that accompanied prior solution attempts of Maria and her parents.]

M: Like, during class?

SP: Yeah, during class, so you can mark it when it happens.

M: (*Smiles.*) Okay, so you want me to count how many mean things she says during class?

SP: Not just the mean things she *says*. Things she *does*, too. She probably does things that are mean, too, doesn't she?

M: Oh yeah.

SP: Okay. So, anything she says or does that's mean, mark it. You could just have a spot on top of the notebook page you're on that day, like this (*demonstrates*). Could you do that this week so we can get a good handle on this?

M: I guess. It's kind of weird (*laughs*). I hope I have enough paper for it (*laughs*).

SP: (*Laughs.*) Yeah. Well, you can make real small marks, as long as you can see them well enough to count them. Another thing. It's important that you not laugh while you're doing this. You don't want to start laughing in class and call attention to what you're doing.

M: (*Smiles.*) Nope. That wouldn't be cool.

SP: No, it wouldn't.

[Her smiles in response to this suggestion indicated a good fit, and prompted an extension of the task to include "not laughing." The "not laughing" component invites a "re-view" of teacher observations from a serious, apprehensive context to a lighter, more humorous one.]

SP: You think you can do this?

M: Yeah. I can do it. There's going to be a lot of marks, though, I'm telling you.

SP: So be it. How about we meet next week to check this out and see how things are going?

M: Okay.

SP: You wanna meet here again?

M: Yeah. That's fine.

This intervention evolved from the practitioner's accommodation of Maria's views on the problem. Lectures and "counseling" had not worked, and a different approach was warranted. Maria eagerly implemented the "observe and record" task during the following week. The results are presented later.

Intervention with Parents

Recall that Maria's parents also were stuck in a problem cycle in which the solution attempts perpetuated the very problem they were intended to resolve. Therefore, the practitioner sought to encourage "something different" that would (1) validate their views of the problem and their desire to remain actively involved, (2) interrupt their solution attempts, and (3) invite them to "view" or "do" something different. The following conversation with Ms. Jordan took place the day after the practitioner's first meeting with Maria.

SP: When we met the first time, you mentioned that the talks you and your husband had with Maria didn't seem to help.

Ms. J: Right. It seems like we're talking to a brick wall. She just shuts down, especially lately.

SP: How willing would you be to try something different?

[This is a useful question when clients express strong frustration with a problem situation, and report that their attempts to resolve it haven't worked well.]

Ms. J: We'll do anything that will help her.

SP: Well, I'd like to get a better handle on how things go this week. I've asked Maria to try something in school. I'll let her tell you, because she wanted to tell you herself instead of having me do it.

Ms. J: (*Smiles.*) She told us about it last night.

SP: Okay. I'd like to ask a favor of you and your husband that's going to take some time and effort, but it might help us get a handle on how things go this week at night and in the mornings and on the way to school.

[This comment frames the suggestion as requiring their active work and effort, which is compatible with their desire to remain involved.]

Ms. J: Okay.

SP: I'd appreciate it if you and your husband could rate her behavior during these times so we can tell when there's change, so we can recognize small improvements when they happen. Okay?

Ms. J: Okay. Sure.

SP: So, if you could rate her behavior every day, we could keep real close track of things. Could you do that?

Ms. J: Sure.

SP: This also will give us a chance to see how Maria does with the school suggestion that she told you about. Plus, it gets you out of the tug-of-war business before your arms fall off. You know, the business of talking to her, her shutting down, and the whole thing upsetting the house like you said.

Ms. J: (*Laughs.*) That sounds good. It's not working anyway.

SP: Exactly. Besides, backing off of talking to her a lot and making suggestions about school might actually give her some confidence. You know, it might convey you and your husband's confidence in her to improve things on her own. Who knows? That could send an important message of support to her.

Ms. J: Yeah. I see what you mean. It's just hard to watch her suffering so much over this.

SP: It's got to be really tough, especially since she's never had any problems like this. It's going to be really hard not to jump in with ideas this week if you decide to do this.

Ms. J: Oh, we'll definitely do it. It makes more sense than what we've been doing.

SP: Well, what you've been doing makes sense. It's just not working with Maria, so we'll take another road and see what happens.

Ms. J: Sounds good.

The practitioner and Ms. Jordan developed a parent rating system for Maria's morning and bedtime behavior, where 1 represented "very unacceptable" and 10 "very acceptable." The parents were asked to "make their best guess" in rating Maria's behavior from the time the problem began about 3 school weeks ago to the present. These ratings would yield a "retrospective baseline" to compare with changes following intervention. Ms. Jordan immediately said "that would be no problem," adding that "they would not have to guess too much" on the ratings because they had major problems almost every day. The parents completed daily ratings of Maria's bedtime and morning behavior for the next 2 months. They also kept track of Maria's requests to have her temperature taken.

The "observe and rate" task was intended to interrupt parents' ineffective attempts to lecture and counsel Maria on the irrationality of her concerns. The practitioner honored the parents' desire to be actively involved and supportive by presenting the suggestion as requiring considerable "time and effort" and "supporting" Maria. The parents diligently completed observations and ratings during the next 2 months.

EVALUATION OF PROGRESS

Progress was evaluated in a second meeting with Maria and subsequent phone contacts with Ms. Jordan. Evaluation also included examination of parent ratings, which Ms. Jordan periodically sent to the practitioner.

Evaluating Progress from Maria's Perspective

The practitioner briefly met with Maria at her house 1 week after their initial meeting. Maria eagerly reported her progress as follows.

M: It's not a problem any more.

SP: What's not a problem?

M: The teacher. School. Everything's snappy.

SP: What do you mean?

M: I'm not nervous about it.

SP: How many marks did you have?

M: (*Opens her notebook and starts counting.*) Oh, let's see. A lot. 97. (*Laughs.*)

SP: 97! (*Laughs.*) Does that surprise you?

M: Not really.

SP: 97 marks for 1 week. Wow. That's some major league meanness. And you're not nervous about it?

M: Nope. I mean, she *is* mean. 97 marks. Give me a break. I'm just not nervous about it anymore.

SP: Where would you rate things on that 1 to 100 scale we talked

about, where 1 is "the total pits," and 100 is "the greatest" it can
be?

M: I'd say about 80.

SP: 80. Wow.

M: Where would you have put it, say, a couple weeks ago?

M: 5 or 10.

SP: Wow. That's quite a change.

M: Yeah.

The remainder of the conversation focused on clarifying and
maintaining Maria's progress. This aspect of the meeting is covered
later.

Evaluating Progress from Parents' Perspective

Parent ratings indicated a marked change in the problem from their
perspective. Maria asked to have her temperature taken on all 15
days prior to intervention (baseline), but only the first 2 of 30 days
following intervention.

The parents completed daily ratings of Maria's morning and
bedtime behavior for 2 months following intervention, and again at
the end of the school year for follow-up purposes. Their daily ratings were averaged on a weekly basis. Parents' postintervention
judgments of the acceptability of Maria's morning and bedtime behavior were compared to baseline ratings using an AB design. The
results are displayed in Figure 8.1. As compared to baseline ratings,
Maria's parents rated her morning and bedtime behavior much
more favorably during the 7 weeks following intervention, and at
follow-up.

MAINTENANCE OF PROGRESS

Once desired changes were reported, the practitioner's focus shifted
toward empowering and maintaining them with Maria and her parents.

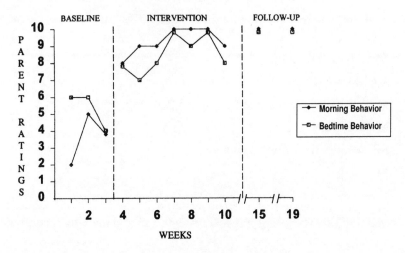

FIGURE 8.1. Parent ratings of the acceptability of Maria's morning and bed-time behavior (1 = very unacceptable, 10 = very acceptable).

Empowering and Maintaining Progress with Maria

The second meeting with Maria lasted about 20 minutes, and re-volved around her description of desired changes. The practitioner seeks to clarify and empower these changes in the following ex-cerpt.

SP: How would you explain this change?

M: I don't know. It just happened. I can't explain it.

SP: How did you manage to do this change?

M: I have no idea. Really. That's all I can say. I told a friend I was coming over to their house after school today. You think we'll be done soon?

[Maria's preference to wrap up the meeting is apparent. The practi-tioner honors this preference in the following dialogue.]

SP: Yeah. We can be done real soon. The only thing I have left to say is that you're on to something here. I don't know what it is, but you're on to something that worked really well for you.

[This statement blames Maria for success by stating that she is "on to something." This statement is intended to (1) promote her owner-ship of desired changes, and (2) allow her the opportunity to con-struct *her own* interpretation of the changes.]

M: I'll say.

SP: Do you want to set another time to meet or just leave it open?

M: Leave it open. I'll tell my parents if I want to meet again. Okay?

SP: That's great. Congratulations. (*Shakes Maria's hand.*)

M: Thanks.

Empowering and Maintaining Progress with Parents

In the next excerpt from a conversation with Ms. Jordan, the practi-tioner employs the following methods of maintaining progress: (1) blaming the parents for success, (2) complimenting the parents on their new approach and inquiring how they resisted the urge to re-turn to the "lecture and counseling" approach, (3) clarifying their plans to maintain desired changes, and (4) "leaving the door open" for booster meetings in the future. This conversation occurred ap-proximately 3 weeks after the desired changes were observed.

SP: I'm really impressed that you've been able to stick to your plan of not lecturing Maria or giving her a lot of advice about the school thing.

Ms. J: Well, it's working, so we're not going to change anything.

SP: Yeah, I know what you mean. Like they say, if it ain't broke, don't fix it, right?

M: (*Laughs.*) Right.

SP: I'm guessing there were times when it was really hard to resist jumping in and giving advice like you used to.

Ms. J: Well, a few times, yeah. She'll say something that almost seems like she's baiting us, you know, trying to push our buttons. (*Laughs.*) Something about the teacher or school. But Paul and I just bite our tongues and that's usually the end of it. We'll say something like, "Well, if that's the way you feel." But there haven't really been that many of those kind of comments lately. It's like she's back to her old self.

SP: It's great that you and Paul have stuck to the plan even in the face of these times when she tries to push your buttons. That's hard to do. Your data collection has also been great. I know how hard it is just to make it through bedtimes and mornings as it is, much less having to do these ratings. You've really helped her by doing all this.

Ms. J: Thank you. I hope so. I just hope things continue like this. Those 3 weeks were bizarre.

SP: Yeah. What are your plans in terms of how you're going to approach things in the future?

Ms. J: Well, we're not going back to those arguments and mini-counseling sessions we tried to have with her. (*Laughs.*) I mean, I'm sure we'll have arguments, like anybody does, but not locking horns like we did where nothing gets done and everybody ends up upset.

SP: Does Paul pretty much feel the same way?

Ms. J: Oh, yeah. He's just happy not to go through almost pulling her from the car in the mornings. Things are normal again.

SP: I know Paul has had to work a lot lately and we haven't had a chance to actually meet or talk on the phone, but please congratulate him for me on these changes.

Ms. J: I will. Thank you.

SP: Congratulations. (*Shakes Ms. Jordan's hand.*)

Ms. J: Thank you for all the help.

SP: You're welcome. In terms of where we go from here, how do you want to handle it?

Ms. J: Well, I guess we don't really need to meet any more, but I'd like to be able to call you if we need to.

SP: Definitely. Call if you think I can help you. Also, I'd appreciate if you could keep track of things a little while longer and I could call you to see how things are going in a few weeks. What do you think about that?

Ms. J: That's fine. These ratings are easy, plus, like you said, we'll be able to see if things keep going well.

SP: Thank you.

The practitioner made two short phone contacts during the last 2 months of the school year to follow up on progress. As previously indicated in Figure 8.1, parent ratings suggested successful maintenance of progress throughout the remainder of the school year.

CONCLUSION AND DISCUSSION

This case highlights the following important features of brief intervention for school problems.

1. The *efficiency and pragmatism* of the approach are illustrated in that assessment and intervention focused only on the persons and interactions seen as directly and currently related to the problem. School personnel were not included because no one at school expressed any concerns whatsoever regarding Maria. No attempt was made to assess areas like family dynamics or personality styles because neither Maria nor her parents indicated interest in, or relevance of, such information. The specific focus of intervention matched their specific request for change.

2. *Each person's theory regarding the problem was accommodated and incorporated into the rationale and content of interventions.* Maria's "mean teacher" position was accommodated by the intervention task of tallying mean marks. The practitioner honored the parents' desire to support Maria and to remain actively involved by presenting the "observe and rate" task as a way of contributing important assessment data and conveying their support and confidence in Maria's ability to develop her own solution.

3. *Interventions were aimed at interrupting existing solution attempts* that contributed to the very problem they were intended to relieve. Ra-

tional counseling, relaxation training, and other "educational" strategies were avoided—*not* because they were seen as inferior to the chosen interventions in some absolute sense, but because *they did not work* with Maria. To paraphrase the chapter's title, "rationality" did not make sense in this case. A very different approach was warranted, based on the intervention guideline, "if at first you don't succeed, try something different."

CHAPTER 9

◆◆◆

Special Challenges
and Final Thoughts

◆

Because we have been full time practitioners, a simple yet crucial point was emphasized throughout this book. Any approach to school problems must be practical, time sensitive, and effective. Too many times we have been disappointed with various approaches that sound great "on paper" or "in the laboratory" but are impractical in the real world. In contrast, brief intervention provides encouragement and optimism because it is both empirical *and* practical.

Although brief intervention is not a panacea for every school problem, we found it to be more effective, and more enjoyable, than other school-based intervention approaches. Allowing students, teachers, and parents to "lead the way" by respecting and accommodating their unique views and skills has expanded the problem-solving process to include new avenues of change. Instead of relying exclusively on our own theories and expertise to resolve school problems, we now utilize students, parents, and teachers as consultants on their own problems. They have proven to be very successful in this role.

SPECIAL CHALLENGES

The "real world" has been our testing ground for the brief intervention approach, and it has passed the test. However, we do not want to imply that rampant euphoria, unbridled success, and a frustration-free professional life await school practitioners who adopt it. Brief intervention is strongly change-focused, and there are several challenges to change in the daily work of school practitioners. These challenges, along with suggestions for dealing with them, are addressed next.

Dealing with Different Positions

As difficult and frustrating as a problem might be to students, parents, and teachers, "doing something different" about it is not as easy as it may sound. Accommodating people's beliefs and values has proven to be a more efficient route to change than trying to dissuade them from their views. Consider the situation in which a teacher or parent holds the attitude, "Why should *I* change when it is the child who has the problem?" This is a common and understandable position. In these cases, we suggest that they might regain control by being less predictable in responding to the problem (Murphy, 1996). This "re-view" invites a different response in a way that validates parents' and teachers' desire for control. Accommodation, therefore, is not just a technique used solely for intervention. Rather, it is an overall style of approaching any challenge faced by school practitioners.

Eligibility versus Intervention

Teachers deal with students day in and day out on their own. Although intervention assistance varies from school to school, things typically get pretty desperate before a teacher initiates a referral. The request may come in the form of a referral for diagnostic evaluation of the student's eligibility for special education services. Teachers' requests for intervention ideas may be secondary to their requests for an eligibility or classification determination. It is difficult to focus on intervention and change in the context of eligibility-driven referrals.

It is also challenging to empower student competencies and resources in the context of evaluation and classification of students. For example, it can be very frustrating for change-focused, competency-oriented school practitioners to sit through eligibility meetings that emphasize "what is wrong" with students and "what to call them," with minimal attention to specific ways of improving their school performance.

These situations are far from ideal for school practitioners who embrace brief intervention and have seen its results. Diagnosis and classification typically focus on a student's deficits, sometimes confirming what is already known and providing minimal direction for change. Labels and attributions often shape our impressions and limit solution opportunities.

Our intent is not to dismiss the benefits of accurate diagnoses, but to highlight the dangers that accompany the *act* of diagnosis and classification. We have found it useful to *expand the diagnostic process* to include assessment of students' competencies. For example, questions about exceptions, prior successes, and other resources can be routinely included in evaluation.

We recommend that the same level of analytical rigor applied to the diagnosis of students' deficiencies be applied to the "diagnosis" of their strengths. Routine assessment of strengths and resources allows the retention of a change focus while approaching eligibility-driven referrals. In the case of Kenny (Chapter 1), successful intervention emerged from a competency-focused interview occurring as part of an eligibility evaluation.

Remaining Solution-Focused versus Solution-Forced

By the time a school practitioner receives a referral, the problem typically has occurred for several weeks or months. As a result, these requests usually are accompanied by a good deal of frustration. There is a tendency in practitioners' initial application of this approach to "force" solutions onto students, parents, and teachers.

As this book has emphasized, efforts to force people into beliefs and actions simply do not work. Coercive tactics impede change and promote the assignment of unproductive labels such as "resistant," "noncompliant," or "uncooperative." In the case of Bonnie and Brandy (Chapter 3), solutions evolved from honoring Bonnie's theory of genetic depression instead of trying to dissuade her from it by imposing a solution-forced framework.

BRIEF INTERVENTION IN A NUTSHELL:
THE 3 C's AND 3 A's

This book presented numerous concepts and techniques. As an aid in summarizing and remembering the core principles and practices of brief intervention, think in terms of the 3 C's and 3 A's. The 3 C's refer to the *change-focused, competency-oriented,* and *client-directed* principles that guide the process of intervention. The 3 A's refer to the key practices of *accepting, acknowledging,* and *accommodating* the students, parents, and teachers with whom we work, along with the goals and perspectives that they bring.

LAST CALL FOR THE CLIENT

> People are generally better persuaded by the
> reasons which they have themselves discovered than
> by those which have come into the minds of others.
> —BLAISE PASCAL

Our experience with school problems has confirmed the adage, "two (or more) heads are better than one," especially when one of them belongs to the person expected to implement interventions. Students, teachers, and parents know themselves and their circumstances better than we ever will. It is easy for them *and* us to lose sight of this in the midst of an overwhelming school problem. As illustrated throughout the book, creative and effective solutions emerge when the opinions and resources of students, parents, and teachers are honored throughout the intervention process.

There is much to be optimistic about. As a profession, we know more now than we ever have about what works. We hope the book has encouraged you and provided some new ideas and techniques that you can apply on the job tomorrow. In the Preface, we stated our hope that you would be "impressed" while reading this book. In closing, we reiterate the hope that you were, and will continue to be, impressed by the resourcefulness of students, parents, and teachers as you work with them in the challenging business of resolving school problems.

APPENDIX

◆◆◆

Useful Interventions

◆

It could be said that there are as many different interventions as there are clients. The inclusion of these suggestions does not mean that they are somehow "better" than others in an absolute sense. They were chosen because (1) they are very useful in promoting *different* views and actions in situations where clients feel stuck and "more of the same" solution attempts prevail, and (2) they come from sources that are unfamiliar to many school practitioners. The source titles, authors and page numbers are listed for each intervention, along with general client descriptions and situations for which the intervention is particularly useful. Many of these interventions were exemplified in this book.

Source: Tactics of Change (Fisch, Weakland, & Segal, 1982)
[*Note:* The titles of Interventions 1, 2, and 3 below describe clients' ineffective solution attempts. The titles of all other interventions describe the intervention itself.]

    Intervention 1. Trying to Force a Response from Oneself That Can Only Occur Spontaneously: Practitioner implicitly asks clients to alter their ineffective solution attempts (attempting to "force" relaxation or sleep) by asking them to perform another behavior that is incompatible with these efforts ("bringing on" anxiety in order to rate it on a scale of 1 to 100) (p.129).
    Client Description/Appropriate Situation. Useful in addressing human performance problems such as anxiety or sleep problems.

Helps client give up unproductive self-coercive attempts to correct problem by voluntary force.

Intervention 2. Attempting to Master a Feared Event by Postponing It. Practitioner designs a task that exposes the student to the feared task, while restraining the student from successfully completing it or improving performance on it (student with a shyness problem is asked to approach a group of peers and not join into the conversation) (p. 136).

Client Description/Appropriate Situation. Useful for students attempting to solve a problem by avoiding the situation (shyness, school phobia/avoidance, writing blocks, etc.). Often accompanied by an assessment rationale in which the practitioner seeks "to learn more about the problem."

Intervention 3. Attempting to Coerce Cooperation from Another. Practitioner urges the client (e.g., teacher, parent) to take a one-down position by making requests in a casual versus authoritarian manner. Often accompanied by the rationale that the parent or teacher has become so "predictable" that the student tunes them out, and that some unpredictability is required to secure their attention and cooperation (p. 139).

Client Description/Appropriate Situation. Useful in dealing with intractable "power struggles" between students and their parents or teachers.

Intervention 4. Go Slow. Practitioner encourages client to do little or nothing, that is, to "go slow" in resolving the problem. Often accompanied by validating rationales including "the challenge of adjusting to sudden and substantial changes," and "the importance of establishing a step-by-step (vs. rushed) foundation for change" (p. 159).

Client Description/Appropriate Situation. Useful for clients who are trying too hard to resolve a problem, or are pressing the practitioner for immediate answers. "Go slow" messages remove the sense of urgency and enable the student, teacher, or parent to relax their problem-maintaining solution attempts. A welcome relief often accompanies the practitioner's suggestions to "go slowly."

Intervention 5. Dangers of Improvement. Practitioner explores with clients the potential dangers or drawbacks associated with resolving the problem (p. 162).

Client Description/Appropriate Situation. Useful in cases of performance anxiety (e.g., test anxiety, shyness, phobia), and for clients who are ambivalent about change or who have struggled with making changes for a long time. This intervention validates the difficulty and challenge inherent in change.

Source: Keys to Solutions in Brief Therapy (de Shazer, 1985)

Intervention 1. Do Something Different. "Between now and the next time we meet, try doing something different when the problem occurs" (p.122).

Client Description/Appropriate Situation. Formula task for any situation in which student, teacher, or parent seems stuck. Accesses client's creative capacities.

Intervention 2. Crystal Ball Technique (Miracle Question). "If a miracle occurred overnight and the problem disappeared, what would things be like for you in school? . . . at home?" (p. 81).

Client Description/Appropriate Situation. Formula task for any situation. Constructs positive expectations for the future. Helps clients clarify their goals.

Intervention 3. Overcoming the Urge. "Pay attention to what you do to overcome the urge to (skip school, talk back to the teacher, hit a student who criticizes you, etc.)" (p. 132).

Client Description/Appropriate Situation. Formula task for any situation in which students, parents, or teachers present a problem about themselves. Enhances client self-efficacy and promotes the discovery of exceptions to the problem that may be elaborated and expanded.

Intervention 4. First-Session Formula Task. "Between now and the next time we meet, observe so that you can describe what happens in school that you would like to continue to have happen" (p. 137).

Client Description/Appropriate Situation. Formula task for any situation. Shifts focus from past to present and future, and promotes expectations of change. Encourages students, parents, and teachers to focus on exceptions that may be amplified.

Source: In Search of Solutions (O'Hanlon & Weiner-Davis, 1989)

Intervention 1. The Surprise Task. "Do at least one or two things that will surprise your teachers/parents. Don't tell them what it is. Parents/teachers, your job is to see if you can tell what it is he/she is doing. Don't compare notes about this" (p. 137).

Client Description/Appropriate Situation. This task introduces randomness and playfulness into intractable problem cycles or patterns, thereby changing the context of the problem from its previous "battle-oriented" quality to a more "game-like" quality. Also enables exceptions to be noted and amplified.

Intervention 2. The Generic Task. Practitioner uses client language to design an intervention that sets up expectancy for change. For example, if a student wants their teachers to "stop hassling them so much," the practitioner suggests, "Keep track of what you are doing this week that seems to make your teachers hassle you less" (p. 138).

Client Description/Appropriate Situation. This task presupposes that desirable "between-meeting" behaviors and events will occur. Allows for exceptions to the problem to be recognized and elaborated.

Source: Overcoming Relationship Impasses (Duncan & Rock, 1991)

Intervention 1. Inviting What You Dread. Practitioner encourages the teacher or parent who is worried about another person's negativism to accept, validate, and even exaggerate the complaints, and to initiate conversation about them (p. 51).

Client Description/Appropriate Situation. Useful when one person (student) is sad, depressed, or pessimistic and verbalizes it frequently, while the other person (parent or teacher) is distressed by the complaints. Interrupts usual solutions of cheerleading and avoiding.

Intervention 2. Agree and Exaggerate. Practitioner suggests the following to a criticized person (e.g., parent): (1) agree in words, but not in action (don't change behavior); (2) don't explain or defend self; and (3) exaggerate criticism in nonsarcastic way (p. 72).

Client Description/Appropriate Situation. Useful for clients who feel controlled and manipulated by another's criticism. Enables disempowered, criticized clients to take charge of their own feelings and of the interaction with the one who criticizes.

Intervention 3. Constructive Payback. Practitioner encourages client (e.g., parent) to attach indirect negative (but harmless) consequence to the chronically irritating behavior (lateness, forgetfulness, etc.) of another person (e.g, student) (p. 86).

Client Description/Appropriate Situation. Indirectly discharges anger and creates conditions for the client's "re-view" of the situation. Particularly useful for parents or teachers dealing with adolescents who persist in grossly inconsiderate behavior despite multiple requests for change. Also injects humor and fun into distressing, tense situations and thereby represents "a difference" that facilitates change.

Intervention 4. Giving Up Power to Gain Effectiveness. Practitioner encourages clients (e.g., teachers) to "give up" the fight verbally, but still be free to do whatever they want behaviorally (e.g., grade the student accordingly) (p. 121).

Client Description/Appropriate Situation. Useful in interrupting ongoing, unproductive verbal battles and power struggles between the student and their parents or teachers.

References

◆

Ajzen, I., & Fishbein, M. (1980). *Understanding attitudes and predicting social behavior.* Englewood Cliffs, NJ: Prentice-Hall.

American Psychiatric Association. (1994). *Diagnostic and statistical manual of mental disorders* (4th ed.). Washington, DC: Author.

Bachelor, A. (1991). Comparison and relationship to outcome of diverse dimensions of the helping alliance as seen by client and therapist. *Psychotherapy, 28,* 534–549.

Bandura, A. (1977). Self-efficacy: Toward a unifying theory of behavior change. *Psychological Review, 84,* 191–215.

Bandura, A. (1986). *Social foundations of thought and action: A social cognitive theory.* Englewood Cliffs, NJ: Prentice-Hall.

Barlow, D. H., Hayes, S. C., & Nelson, R. O. (1984). *The scientist–practitioner: Research and accountability in clinical and educational settings.* Elmsford, NY: Pergamon Press.

Berg, I. K. (1991). *Family preservation: A brief therapy workbook.* London: Brief Therapy Press.

Berg, I. K., & Miller, S. D. (1992). *Working with the problem drinker: A solution-focused approach.* New York: Norton.

Bergan, J. R., & Kratochwill, T. R. (1990). *Behavioral consultation and therapy.* New York: Plenum Press.

Bergin, A. E. (1971). The evaluation of therapeutic outcome. In A. E. Bergin & S. L. Garfield (Eds.), *Handbook of psychotherapy and behavior change* (pp. 217–270). New York: Wiley.

Bergin, A. E., & Lambert, M. J. (1978). The evaluation of therapeutic outcomes. In S. L. Garfield & A. E. Bergin (Eds.), *Handbook of psychotherapy and behavior change* (2nd ed., pp. 139–190). New York: Wiley.

Bordin, E. S. (1979). The generalizability of the psychoanalytic concept of the working alliance. *Psychotherapy, 16,* 252–260.

Brigham, T. A. (1989). *Self-management for adolescents: A skills-training program.* New York: Guilford Press.

Cade, B., & O'Hanlon, W. H. (1993). *A brief guide to brief therapy.* New York: Norton.

Conoley, C. W., Ivey, D., Conoley, J. C., Scheel, M., & Bishop, R. (1992). Enhancing consultation by matching the consultee's perspectives. *Journal of Counseling Development, 69,* 546–549.

Coyne, J. C. (1986). The significance of the interview in strategic marital therapy. *Journal of Strategic and Systemic Therapies, 5,* 63–70.

de Shazer, S. (1985). *Keys to solutions in brief therapy.* New York: Norton.

de Shazer, S. (1991). *Putting difference to work.* New York: Norton.

Duncan, B. L. (1989). Paradoxical procedures in family therapy. In L. M. Ascher (Ed.), *Therapeutic paradox* (pp. 310–348). New York: Guilford Press.

Duncan, B. L., Hubble, M. A., & Miller, S. D. (1997). *Psychotherapy with impossible cases.* New York: Norton.

Duncan, B. L., & Moynihan, D. W. (1994). Applying outcome research: Intentional utilization of the client's frame of reference. *Psychotherapy, 31*(2), 294–302.

Duncan, B. L., & Rock, J. W. (1991). *Overcoming relationship impasses: Ways to initiate change when your partner won't help.* New York: Insight.

Duncan, B. L., Solovey, A. D., & Rusk, G. S. (1992). *Changing the rules: A client-directed approach to therapy.* New York: Guilford Press.

Durrant, M. (1995). *Creative strategies for school problems.* New York: Norton.

Durrant, M., & Kowalski, K. M. (1995). Enhancing views of competence. In S. Friedman (Ed.), *The new language of change: Constructive collaboration in psychotherapy* (pp. 107–137). New York: Guilford Press.

Elkin, I., Shea, T., Watkins, J. T., Imber, S. D., Sotsky, S. M., Collins, I. F., Glass, D. R., Pilkonis, P. A., Leber, W. R., Dockerty, J. P., Fiester, S. J., & Parloff, M. B. (1989). National Institute of Mental Health Treatment of Depression Collaborative Research Program: General effectiveness of treatments. *Archives of General Psychiatry, 46,* 971–982.

Elliot, S. N. (1988). Acceptability of behavioral treatments: Review of variables that influence treatment selection. *Professional Psychology: Research and Practice, 19,* 68–80.

Elliot, S. N., Witt, J. C., Galvin, G., & Peterson, R. (1984). Acceptability of behavioral interventions: Factors that influence teachers' decisions. *Journal of School Psychology, 22,* 353–360.

Fisch, R., Weakland, J. H., & Segal, L. (1982). *The tactics of change: Doing therapy briefly.* San Francisco: Jossey-Bass.

Frank, J. D. (1976). Psychotherapy and the sense of mastery. In R. L. Spitzer & D. F. Klein (Eds.), *Evaluation of psychotherapies: Behavioral therapies, drug therapies and their interactions* (pp. 47–56). Baltimore: Johns Hopkins Press.

Frank, J. D., & Frank, J. B. (1991). *Persuasion and healing* (3rd ed.). Baltimore: Johns Hopkins Press.

Garfield, S. L. (1994). Research on client variables in psychotherapy. In A. E. Bergin & S. L. Garfield (Eds.), *Handbook of psychotherapy and behavior change* (4th ed., pp. 190–228). New York: Wiley.

Goleman, D. (1991, December 24). In new research, optimism emerges as the key to successful life. *New York Times*, pp. B5–B6.

Gravetter, F. J., & Wallnau, L. B. (1992). *Statistics for the behavioral sciences* (3rd ed.). St. Paul, MN: West.

Gurman, A. S. (1977). Therapist and patient factors influencing the patient's perception of facilitative therapeutic conditions. *Psychiatry, 40,* 16–24.

Gutkin, T. B., & Curtis, M. J. (1990). School-based consultation: Theory, techniques, and research. In T. B. Gutkin & C. R. Reynolds (Eds.), *The handbook of school psychology* (2nd ed., pp. 577–611). New York: Wiley.

Haley, J. (1987). *Problem-solving therapy* (2nd ed.). San Francisco: Jossey-Bass.

Heath, A. W., & Atkinson, B. J. (1989). Solutions attempted and considered: Broadening assessment in brief therapy. *Journal of Strategic and Systemic Therapies, 8,* 56–57.

Horowitz, M., Marmar, C., Weiss, D., DeWitt, K., & Rosenbaum, R. (1984). Brief psychotherapy of bereavement reactions: The relationship of process to outcome. *Archives of General Psychiatry, 41,* 438–448.

Howard, K., Kopta, M., Krause, M., & Orlinsky, D. (1986). The dose–effect relationship in psychotherapy. *American Psychologist, 41,* 149–164.

Imber, S. D., Pilkonis, P. A., Harway, N. I., Klein, R. H., & Rubinsky, P. A. (1982). Maintenance of change in the psychotherapies. *Journal of Psychiatric Treatment and Evaluation, 4,* 1–5.

Kaminer, W. (1992). *I'm dysfunctional, you're dysfunctional.* New York: Addison–Wesley.

Kazdin, A. E. (1980). Acceptability of alternative treatments for deviant child behavior. *Journal of Applied Behavior Analysis, 13,* 259–273.

Kazdin, A. E. (1994). *Behavior modification in applied settings.* Pacific Grove, CA: Brooks/Cole.

Kelley, M. L. (1990). *School–home notes: Promoting children's classroom success.* New York: Guilford Press.

Kottler, J. A. (1991). *The compleat therapist.* San Francisco: Jossey-Bass.

Kowalski, K., & Kral, R. (1989). The geometry of solution: Using the scaling technique. *Family Therapy Case Studies, 4,* 59–66.

Kral, R. (1986). Indirect therapy in the schools. In S. de Shazer & R. Kral (Eds.), *Indirect approaches in therapy* (pp. 56–63). Rockville, MD: Aspen.

Kratochwill, T. R., & Bergan, J. R. (1990). *Behavioral consultation in applied settings: An individual guide.* New York: Plenum Press.

Lafferty, P., Beutler, L. E., & Crago, M. (1989). Differences between more and less effective psychotherapists: A study of selected therapist variables. *Journal of Consulting and Clinical Psychology, 57,* 76–80.

Lambert, M. J. (1992). Implications of outcome research for psychotherapy integration. In J. C. Norcross & M. R. Goldfried (Eds.), *Handbook of psychotherapy integration* (pp. 94–129). New York: Basic Books.

Lambert, M. J., & Bergin, A. E. (1994). The effectiveness of psychotherapy. In A. E. Bergin & S. L. Garfield (Eds.), *Handbook of psychotherapy and behavior change* (4th ed., pp. 143–189). New York: Wiley.

Lawson, D. (1994). Identifying pretreatment change. *Journal of Counseling and Development, 72*, 244–248.

Luborsky, L., Singer, B., & Luborsky, L. (1975). Comparative studies of psychotherapies: Is it true that "everybody has won and all must have prizes"? *Archives of General Psychiatry, 32*, 995–1008.

Madanes, C. (1981). *Strategic family therapy.* San Francisco: Jossey-Bass.

Madden, T. J., Ellen, P. S., & Ajzen, I. (1992). A comparison of the theory of planned behavior and the theory of reasoned action. *Personality and Social Psychology Bulletin, 18*, 3–9.

Mahoney, M. J. (1991). *Human change processes: The scientific foundations of psychotherapy.* New York: Basic Books.

Marmar, C., Horowitz, M. J., Weiss, D. S., & Marziali, E. (1986). The development of the Therapeutic Alliance Rating System. In L. S. Greenberg & W. N. Pinsof (Eds.), *The psychotherapeutic process: A research handbook* (pp. 367–390). New York: Guilford Press.

Miller, S., & Berg, I. (1994). *The miracle method: A radically new approach to problem drinking.* New York: Norton.

Miller, S. D., Duncan, B. L., & Hubble, M. A. (1997). *Escape from Babel: Toward a unifying language for psychotherapy practice.* New York: Norton.

Miller, S. D., Hubble, M. A., & Duncan, B. L. (1996). *Handbook of solution-focused brief therapy: Research, theory, and practice.* San Francisco: Jossey-Bass.

Murphy, J. J. (1996). Solution-focused brief therapy in the school. In S. D. Miller, M. A. Hubble, & B. L. Duncan (Eds.), *Handbook of solution-focused brief therapy: Research, theory, and practice* (pp. 184–204). San Francisco: Jossey-Bass.

Murphy, P. M., Cramer, D., & Lillie, F. J. (1984). The relationship between curative factors perceived by patients in their psychotherapy and treatment outcome: An exploratory study. *British Journal of Medical Psychology, 57*, 187–192.

O'Hanlon, W. H. (1987). *Taproots: Underlying principles of Milton H. Erickson's therapy and hypnosis.* New York: Norton.

O'Hanlon, W. H., & Weiner-Davis, M. (1989). *In search of solutions: A new direction in psychotherapy.* New York: Norton.

Orlinsky, D. E., Grawe, K., & Parks, B. K. (1994). Process and outcome in psychotherapy—noch einmal. In A. E. Bergin, & S. L. Garfield (Eds.), *Handbook of psychotherapy and behavior change* (4th ed., pp. 270–376). New York: Wiley.

Orlinsky, D. E., & Howard, K. I. (1986). Process and outcome in psychotherapy. In S. L. Garfield & A. E. Bergin (Eds.), *Handbook of psychotherapy and behavior change* (3rd ed., pp. 311–381). New York: Wiley.

Parry, A. (1991). A universe of stories. *Family Process, 30,* 37–54.

Patterson, C. H. (1984). Empathy, warmth, and genuineness in psychotherapy: A review of reviews. *Psychotherapy, 21,* 431–438.

Patterson, C. H. (1989). Foundations for an eclectic psychotherapy. *Psychotherapy, 26,* 427–435.

Reinking, R. H., Livesay, G., & Kohl, M. (1978). The effects of consultation style on consultee productivity. *American Journal of Community Psychology, 6,* 283–290.

Reuterlov, H., Lofgren, T., Nordstrom, K., & Ternstrom, A. (in press). What's better?: Client's reports of change in second and subsequent sessions. *Brief Therapy.*

Rosenfield, I. (1988). *The invention of memory.* New York: Basic Books.

Selvini-Palazzoli, M., Boscolo, L., Cecchin, G., & Prata, G. (1978). *Paradox: A new model in the therapy of the family in schizophrenic transaction.* New York: Jason Aronson.

Sloane, R. B., Staples, F. R., Cristol, A. H., Yorkston, N. J., & Whipple, K. (1975). *Psychotherapy versus behavior therapy.* Cambridge, MA: Harvard University Press.

Smith, M. L., Glass, G. V., & Miller, T. I. (1980). *The benefits of psychotherapy.* Baltimore: Johns Hopkins Press.

Snyder, C. R., Irving, L. M., & Anderson, J. R. (1991). Hope and health. In C. R. Snyder & D. R. Forsyth (Eds.), *Handbook of social and clinical psychology: The health perspective* (pp. 285–305). Elmsford, NY: Pergamon Press.

Walter, J. L., & Peller, J. E. (1992). *Becoming solution-focused in brief therapy.* New York: Brunner/Mazel.

Watzlawick, P. (1987). *The language of change.* New York: Norton.

Watzlawick, P., Weakland, J., & Fisch, R. (1974). *Change: Principles of problem formation and problem resolution.* New York: Norton.

Weakland, J. H., & Fisch, R., (1992). Brief therapy: MRI style. In S. H,. Budman, M. F. Hoyt, & S. Friedman (Eds.), *The first session in brief therapy* (pp. 306–323). New York: Guilford Press.

Weakland, J. H., Fisch, R., Watzlawick, P., & Bodin, A. M. (1974). Brief therapy: Focused problem resolution. *Family Process, 13,* 141–168.

Webster's Collegiate Dictionary (10th ed.). (1993). New York: Merriam Webster.

Weiner-Davis, M., de Shazer, S., & Gingerich, W. (1987). Using pretreatment change to construct a therapeutic solution: An exploratory study. *Journal of Marital and Family Therapy, 13*(4), 359–363.

Wexler, D. B. (1991). *The adolescent self.* New York: Norton.

White, M., & Epston, D. (1990). *Narrative means to therapeutic ends.* New York: Norton.

Wolf, M. M. (1978). Social validity: The case for subjective measurement, or how applied behavior analysis is finding its heart. *Journal of Applied Behavior Analysis, 11,* 203–214.

Index

♦

AB design, 92, 147
Acceptance, 8
  definition of, 138
  vs. agreement, 138
Accommodate, definition of, 10
Accommodation
  of client goals, 11, 117, 151
  of client's frame of reference,
    27–36, 143, 154
  definition of, 28
  in intervention tasks, 11–12
  of relationship, 11
Adolescents
  independence and, 117
  motivation of, 117
  power plays and, 117
Agree and exaggerate intervention,
    72–73, 161
Agreement, as intervention, 72–73
Alliance, 9–11, 117, 132
  characteristics of, 10
  client perceptions of, 9–10, 14
  lack of, 18–19
  research on, 9–10
Anxiety, 157
Arguing, redefinition of, 82
Assertive discipline, 74–75
Assessment
  first interviews in, 27–43, 131–139
  as a term, 28
Assignment, 92
Assumptions, limitations of, 22–23

Attention, attracting, 67
Avoidance
  interruption of, 69
  school, 158

B

Background
Beginner's mind, 63
Behavior
  classroom, 8
  grossly inconsiderate, 161
  new approaches to, 68
Behavioral plans, statement of, 103
Behavioral sequences, 112
Beliefs, limitations of, 22–23
Between-meeting change, 47–48, 160
Blaiming clients for success, 95–100
Booster meetings, 105–106

C

Caring, 10
Case examples
  Alice, Steve, and Jill, 58–60
  Angelique, 100–103
  Bonnie and Brandy, 29–36, 39–40,
    41, 70–74, 155
  David, Beth, and Adam, 41–42,
    74–79
  Dottie and Jermaine, 55–58
  Eileen and Max, 37
  Greg, 98–100
  James and Ms. Walters, 105–106

Jamie, 23–24
Joshua, 103
Kathleen, 20–21
Kenny, 3–5, 155
Larry, 109–129
Leslie, 38
Maria, 130–152
Mark, 83–85
Michael, 8
Mildred and Jimmy, 34
Molly, 7–8, 15–20
Mr. Carroll and Steven, 103–104
Ms. Walters and James, 105–106
Peg, Dan, and Sam, 81–82
Rachelle, 96–97
Challenges, 153–156
Change(s)
    clarifying client role in, 98–100
    client ownership of, 48–49, 142–143
    client reflection on, 103
    client role in, 45
    in interventions, 62–86
    between meeting, 47–48
    preintervention, 46–47
    in problem patterns, 66–67, 112
    promotion of, 49–50
    rapidity of, 5
    small, 5, 122
    statements of plans for, 103
Change factors, 6–14
    client, 6–8
    model, 6–7, 13–14
    placebo, 6–7, 12–13
    relationship, 6–7, 8–12
Change focus
    cultivating, 46–50
    definition of, 46
Checklists, 90
Classification
    act of, 155
    of students, 154–155
Client
    frame of reference of, 27–36
    in positive outcome, 45
    validation of, 38–40, 41, 132
Client competencies, recognition of,
    49–50
Client factors, 6–8, 14, 44–61, 129
    between-meeting change in, 47–48,
    160

change focus and, 46–50
    definition of, 7
    preintervention change in, 46–47
    recognition of, 45–50
Client goals, accommodating, 11, 117,
    151
Client incompetence, cult of, 44
Client knows best intervention, 14,
    15–20, 44–61, 130
    case example of, 15–20
    recognizing client factors in, 45–50
Client participation, process outcome
    and, 10
Clients, content generated by, 82–83
Client's theory of change, validation
    of, 69, 73, 112–113, 136
Coercive solutions, avoidance of, 75
Coercive tactics, 155, 158
Collaboration
    in achieving goals, 9, 117
    components of, 93
    in goal formulation, 116–117, 122
    as maintenance strategy, 93–95
    one-down style of, 93–95, 132, 142,
    158
Common sense recipe, 14–24
Competencies, client, 5
    recognition of, 49–50
Conditions, for client to change, 9
Conflict negotiation, 75
Confrontive solutions, avoidance of, 75
Constructive payback, 75–76, 77–78,
    161
Content, client generation of, 82–83
Controlling, redefinition of, 82
Conversation, as a term, 28
Cooperation, coercing, 158
Cooperative stance, 116
Coping styles, 20
Counselor
    beneficial influence of, 9
    client perceptions of, 9
    effective role of, 10
    qualities of, 8–10
Credibility, counselor, 12
Criticism, new approaches to, 68
Criticized clients, 161
Crystal ball technique, 159
3 C's and 3 A's, 156
Cumulative files, student, 92

D

Data, permanent product, 90, 92
Defiance, new approaches to, 68
Defiant, redefinition of, 83
Diagnosis
   act of, 155
   assessing competencies in, 155
Diathesis–stress paradigm, 71
Difficulties, problems from, 21, 62
Discipline
   assertive, 74–75
   records of, 90, 92
Disempowered clients, 161
Doing more of the same, 62–63
Do something different strategy, 63–79,
      116, 130, 144, 154, 159
Dread, inviting what you, 160

E

Effectiveness, counselor, 9
Efficiency, 151
Elaborating, 52–53, 54, 55–56, 117,
      118–121
Eliciting, 51–52, 54, 55–56, 117,
      118–119
Eligibility, *vs.* intervention, 154–155
Emotional involvement, 10
Empathy, 8
   accurate, 9
Empirical foundations, 6–24
Empirical validity, 88
Empowering, 53, 54, 57–58, 59–60,
      118, 124, 127–128
   client, 94, 100–103, 124, 127–128
   client plans, 100–103
   from owning change, 48–49, 124,
      127–128
Encouragement, of risk taking, 8
Evaluation, 53, 54, 118
   of progress, 87–93, 123
   of students, 154–155
Exaggeration, as intervention, 72–73
Exceptions, 36–37
   definition of, 50
   five-E method for, 50–60, 114, 118,
      129
   frequency of, 53
   other contexts of, 53
Expanding, 53, 54, 57, 59–60,

117–118, 121–122
Expectancy, 12
Experience, past, 22–23
Exploring, client plans, 100–103

F

Families, interviewing, 40–42
First-session formula tasks, 52,
      159–160
Five-E method
   advantages of, 60–61
   case example of, 117–118
   elaborating in, 52–53, 54, 55–56,
      117, 118–121
   eliciting in, 51–52, 54, 55–56, 117,
      118–119
   empowering in, 53, 54, 57–58,
      59–60, 118, 124, 127–128
   evaluation in, 53, 54, 118
   expanding in, 53, 54, 57, 59–60,
      117–118, 121–122
   practical implications of, 60–61, 123
Forced response, 157–158
Formula tasks, first-session, 52,
      159–160
Fortuitous events, 8
Frame of reference, client, 27–36
   characteristics of, 29

G

Generic task, 160
Genuineness, 9
Giving up power, 75–76, 78, 161
Goal attainment, assessment of, 53
Goal formulation
   client-directed, 117
   collaborative, 117
Goals, client, 34–36, 117, 140–141
   accommodating, 11, 117, 151
   small, 34–36, 122
Go slow technique, 158
Grade books, 92

H

Habits, resisting, 98
Help, 10
Homework assignments, 92
Homework completion, case example
      of, 98–100
Hope, 12

I

Immaturity, redefinition of, 83
Improvement
    dangers of, 159
    early, 47
    predictors of, 9
    at termination, preintervention
        change and, 47
Impulsive, redefinition of, 83
Interpretations, presenting, 95
Interrupting, of solution attempts,
    65–68, 141, 144, 151–152
Intervention(s)
    change in, 62–86
    client customizing, 65
    client knows best, 14, 15–20, 44–61,
        130
    definition of, 64
    designing, 65–79
    developing and selecting, 65
    faith in, 13
    family, 40–42
    as invention, 64
    material for, 4
    presenting, 65
    questions for designing, 65
    student as consultant in, 4–5, 8
    useful, 157–161
    vs. eligibility, 154–155
Intervention(s), effective
    empirical foundations of, 6–24
    function of, 8
    recipe for, 14–24
    research on, 6–24
Intervention change
    do something different strategy,
        63–79, 116, 130, 144, 154, 159
    view something different strategy,
        63, 79–85, 143–144
Intervention failure, causes of, 34
Intervention goals, agreement on, 10
Intervention pie, 7–14
Intervention process, client perceptions
    of, 9
Intervention tasks, agreement on, 10,
    11–12
Interview
    client, in Larry's case, 115–121
    client as controller of, 29
    client's frame of reference in, 27–36

    objectives of, 36
    purpose of, 27
Interview, first, 27–43
    client's frame of reference in, 27–36
    client's theory of change in, 29–36,
        112–113, 134–136
    discovering possibilities in, 36–38
    of families, 40–42
    of family members, separate, 40–41
    MRI elements of, 30
Interviewing, as a term, 28
Intractability, in problem solving, 63
Invention
    definition of, 64
    intervention as, 64, 65
Inventories, 90
Involvement, emotional, 10

L

Leaving the door open, 94, 104–106,
    127, 149, 150–151

M

Madanes model, 82
Maintenance, of progress, 87, 93–106
Maintenance strategies
    blaming clients for success, 95–100
    collaborating, 93–95
    empowering clients' plans, 100–103
    helping clients prepare for relapse,
        103–104
    leaving the door open, 104–106
    qualities of, 93
Meanings, new, discovery of, 37–38
Memory, reinterpretation of, 37–38
Mental Research Institute
    on interview elements, 30
    problem development model of, 20
Midterm progress reports, 92
Mind, beginner's, 63
Model factors, 6–7, 13–14
    definition of, 13

N

Negotiation, 75
Nine-dot problem, 21–24

O

Observation tasks, to interrupt prob-
    lem patterns, 68, 113–114,

141–146, 151–152
One-down collaborative style, 93–95,
  132, 142, 158
Open door, 94, 104–106, 127, 149,
  150–151
Ordeal, creating, 67
Outcome
  preintervention change and, 47
  successful, factors in, 6–7
Outcome research, relationship factors
  in, 9, 10
Outcome studies, model role in, 13–14
Outcome success, client role in, 45
Ownership
  of change, 48–49, 53, 142–143

P

Paper-and-pencil methods, 90
Parents, as intervention consultants, 5,
  8
Participation, client, process outcome
  and, 10
Passive, redefinition of, 83
Pattern interrupters, 65–68, 112
Patterns, resisting, 98
Performance problems, 157
Permanent product data, 90, 92
Personal agency, enhancing, 95
Pessimistic clients, 160
Phobia, school, 158, 159
Placebo factors, 6–7, 12–13
  application of, 12–13
  definition of, 12
Possibilities, discovery of, 36–38
Postponing, 158
Power plays, 117
Power struggles, 158, 161
Practical validity, 88, 123
Pragmatism, 151
Preintervention change, 46–47
Pride, client, 17, 20
Problem cycle
  alteration of, 65–66, 143–144
  vicious, 138
Problem development, Mental Re-
  search Institute model of, 20, 62
Problem patterns
  changes in, 65–68, 112
  characteristics of, 65–66
Problem(s)

alternative view of, 80, 144
client description of, 51–52,
  112–113, 132–134
client's view of, 30–31, 112–113,
  132–134
constancy of, 51–52
defining, 30–31
description of, 111, 133–134
development of, 21, 62
exceptions to, 32–33, 114, 118, 129
intractability of, 63
linking of, to undesirable activity, 67
nine-dot, 21–24
questions to elucidate, 31–32
reframing of, 79–80
re-viewing of, 80, 143, 154, 161
selecting useful view of, 80–81
solution as, 21
Problem–solution cycle, 63
Progress
  evaluating, 87–93
    methods for, 89–92
    practicality of, 92–93, 123
    timing of, 87–88
  maintaining, 87, 93–106
    booster meetings in, 106
    case examples of, 98–100,
      101–103, 123–128, 147–151
    questions to help in, 100–103
    strategies for, 93–106
Progress reports, midterm, 92

Q

Questions
  to ask in scaling, 90, 91, 137
  based on exceptions and solutions,
    36–37
  for designing intervention, 65
  in direction and success of interview,
    36
  to elaborate exceptions, 52, 118–
    121
  to elicit exceptions, 51–52, 114, 118
  to explore complaint, 31
  to explore problem exceptions, 33,
    114
  to explore solution attempts, 33, 114
  to formulate small goals, 35,
    121–122
  to maintain progress, 100–103

R

Rebellion-inducing methods, 75
Reclusive, redefinition of, 83
Reframing
    definition of, 79–80
    of problem, 79–80
Regression effect, 47
Relapse
    discussing possibility of, 104
    preparing client for, 94, 103–104
Relationship, client perception of, 11
Relationship bond, 10
Relationship factors, 6–7, 8–12, 129
    client perceptions of, 9
    definition of, 8–9
    as predictors of improvement, 9
    research on, 9
Report cards, 90, 92
Resources, client, 5, 49–50. *See also*
    Client factors
Respect, 9
Reversal design, 92
Re-viewing problems, 80, 82, 154, 161
    case examples of, 82–85, 143
Rigidity, redefinition of, 83
Risk taking, encouragement of, 8

S

Sad clients, 160
Scaling, 89–90
    application of, 89–90, 137–138, 141,
        145, 146–147
    definition of, 89
    questions to ask in, 90, 91, 137
Scaling techniques, 53
Self-efficacy
    enhancing, 95, 159
    owning change and, 48–49
Self-empowering, 37
Self-esteem, enhancing, 17
Setbacks, creative response to, 104
Shyness, 158, 159
Single-case designs, 92
Sleep problems, 157
Social validity, 88–89, 123
Solution(s)
    client, 17, 112–113
    exploration of, 32–34
    as problem, 21
Solution attempts, 32–33, 36–37, 138,

        140
    interruption of, 65–68, 69, 73,
        75–76, 141, 144, 151–152
Solution-focused, *vs.* solution-forced,
    155–156
Solution orientation, 63
Strategic orientation, 63
Student factors. *See* Client factors
Students, as intervention consultants,
    4–5
Success
    "blaming" clients for, 94, 95–100,
        124, 127–128, 148–149, 149–150
    clarifying cause of, 97–98
    existing, increasing, 50–51
    reflecting on, 97–98
Suggestions, offering tentatively, 95,
    121
Surprise task, 160

T

Tasks
    formula, first-session, 52, 159–160
    generic, 160
    observation, 68, 113–114, 141–146,
        151–152
    surprise, 160
Teachers, as intervention consultants,
    5, 8
Test anxiety, 159
Theory of change, client, 29–36,
    112–113, 134–136
    accommodation of, 29
    case example of, 29–36
    elements of, 29
Time-series designs, 92
Transitions, problems with, 20
Try something different intervention,
    62–86, 144, 154

U

Unpredictability, 68
Urge, overcoming, 159

V

Validation
    of client, 38–40, 41
    of client change, 46
    of client's experience, 69–70, 73–74,
        78–79, 132

of client's theory of change, 69, 73, 112–113, 134–136

Validity
  empirical, 88
  practical, 88, 123
  social, 88–89, 123
  threats to, internal, 92

Vicious problem cycle, 138, 143–144

View, different, 79–85
  reframing problem in, 79–80
  re-viewing problem in, 80, 82–85, 143, 154, 161
  selection of, 80–82
  theoretical approaches in, 80–82

View something different strategy, 63, 79–85, 144

W

Warmth, 8–9, 10
Withdrawn, redefinition of, 83
Work samples, 92
Writing block, 158